C000284273

LAUGHING WILD

BY CHRISTOPHER DURANG

DRAMATISTS
PLAY SERVICE
INC.

LAUGHING WILD
Copyright © Revised 1996, Christopher Durang
Copyright © 1988, Christopher Durang

LAUGHING WILD was presented by Playwrights Horizons (Andre Bishop, Artistic Director and Paul S. Daniels, Executive Director) on October 23, 1987. It was directed by Ron Lagomarsino; the set design was by Thomas Lynch; the costume design was by William Ivey Long; the lighting design was by Arden Fingerhut; the sound design was by Stan Metelits; the press representative was Bob Ullman; the production manager was Carl Mulert; and the production stage manager was M. A. Howard. The cast was as follows:

ACT I

1. LAUGHING WILD
   Woman. . . . . .E. Katherine Kerr
2. SEEKING WILD
   Man. . . . . Christopher Durang

ACT II

3. DREAMING WILD
   Woman. . . . . .E. Katherine Kerr
   Man. . . . . Christopher Durang

Author's Note Regarding Title

The phrase "laughing wild" occurs in Samuel Beckett's *Happy Days,* in which Winnie, who's always trying to remember her "classics" says: "Oh, well, what does it matter, that is what I always say, so long as one . . . you know . . . what is that wonderful line . . . laughing wild . . . something something laughing wild amid severest woe."

Beckett and Winnie in turn are quoting Thomas Gray and his poem "Ode on a Distant Prospect of Eton College," in which the "something something" is "and moody Madness laughing wild amid severest woe."

LAUGHING WILD

1. LAUGHING WILD

SCENE

A Woman enters and addresses the audience.

She should be dressed fairly normally. She sits in a chair and talks to the audience. She can get up from the chair from time to time if the spirit moves her.

The backdrop behind her should be nondescript—pretty much a limbo setting.

WOMAN. Oh, it's all such a mess. Look at this mess. My hair is a mess. My clothes are a mess.

I want to talk to you about life. It's just too difficult to be alive, isn't it, and to try to function? There are all these people to deal with. I tried to buy a can of tuna fish in the supermarket, and there was this *person* standing right in front of where I wanted to reach out to get the tuna fish, and I waited a while, to see if they'd move, and they didn't —they were looking at tuna fish too, but they were taking a real long time on it, reading the ingredients on each can like they were a book, a pretty boring book, if you ask me, but nobody has; so I waited a long while, and they didn't move, and I couldn't get to the tuna fish cans; and I thought about asking them to move, but then they seemed so stupid not to have *sensed* that I needed to get by them that I had this awful fear that it would do no good, no good at all, to ask them, they'd probably say something like, "We'll move when we're goddam ready, you nagging bitch," and then what would I do? And so then I started to cry out of frustration, quietly, so as not to disturb anyone, and still, even though I was softly sobbing, this stupid person didn't *grasp* that I needed to get by them to reach the goddam tuna fish, people are so insensitive, I just hate them, and so I reached over with my fist, and I brought it down real hard on his head and I screamed: "Would you kindly, move, asshole!!!"

And the person fell to the ground, and looked totally startled, and some child nearby started to cry, and I was still crying, and I couldn't imagine making use of the tuna fish now anyway, and so I shouted at the child to stop crying—I mean, it was drawing too much attention to me—and I ran out of the supermarket, and I thought, I'll take a taxi to the Metropolitan Museum of Art, I need to be surrounded with culture right now, not tuna fish.

But you know how hard it is to hail a taxi. I waved my hand, and then this terrible man who came to the street *after* I was there waved his hand, and the taxi stopped for him because he saw him first, and the injustice of it made my eyes start to well with tears again. So I lost that taxi. So I raised my hand again, and the next *three* taxis were already full, although one of them still had his "free" light on which made me angry, because if he had had it off, I probably wouldn't have raised my arm, which was getting tired now, I think hitting the man with the tuna fish used some muscles I wasn't used to using. And then this other taxi started to get near, and this woman with groceries came out, and she started to hail it and I went right over to her and I shouted smack into her ear: "If you take this taxi from me, I will kill you!" And she looked really startled, and then the taxi stopped, and I got in, and I said, I want to go crosstown to the Metropolitan Museum of Art, I must have culture, and quiet, and things of value around me, I have had a terrible time in the supermarket. And then the taxi driver, who was Greek or Muslim or Armenian or something, said to me, I have to go *down*town now, I'm about to get off work.

Well, I thought my head would explode. I mean, was his taxi available, or wasn't it? And wasn't it *law* that they can't refuse you, even if you want to go to Staten Island? But I just couldn't bear the thought of pressing charges against this man — it would take days and days of phone calls, and meetings, and letters, and all because he wouldn't bring me to the goddam Metropolitan. So I sat in his taxi and I wouldn't move. I thought for a while about going back and following through on my initial impulse to buy a can of tuna fish — tuna fish, mixed with mayonnaise, is one of the few things I can make in the kitchen — but then I realized that probably whoever was at the cash register would give me difficulties, probably because I was a woman, or because she was a woman, or maybe it was a man who hated women, or wished he was a woman — anyway it all started to seem far too complicated; so I thought, I'll just stay in this taxi cab, and I'll be damned if I get out. And he kept saying, "Lady, please, I have to get home to my family." And I said "Where? In Staten Island?"

And then I thought, I won't even argue, I'll just sit here. And he started to shout at me, obscenities and so on, and I thought, well, at least I'm sitting down; maybe eventually he'll decide it's easier just to drive me to the Metropolitan; although I started to think maybe I didn't want to go there anyway, I was hungry, for starters, maybe a movie with popcorn and diet Coke and those chocolate-covered ice-cream balls, what are they called — they're delicious, and they cost about $2.50 in the movie theatre, which is ridiculously expensive, but then what movie would I see; and then all of a sudden he pulled his cab out into traffic in a great big hurry, it made me sort of lurch in my seat, and I yelled out, "I've changed my mind, I want to see a movie;" and before I could ask him for recommendations, he said he was taking me to the police station, and I thought, yes, but isn't he in the wrong, refusing a fare? But then you know the stories you've read about police brutality and all, maybe they'd have one of those electrical devices, and they'd shock me even though I wasn't Puerto Rican — well, whatever, I didn't think going to the police was worth it as a risk, so when he stopped at a stop light — violently, I might add, there's probably something wrong with my back, I could sue, but litigation is so complicated and here I can't even buy a can of tuna — I swung the cab door open and I shouted into his open window, "Your mother sucks cocks in hell!" Although I think my tongue slipped and I actually said "Your mother sucks *socks* in hell," which was kind of funny, but I was too angry to laugh; and he just said, "you're fuckin' nuts," and he drove off in this terrible hurry, and the tire almost went over my foot, but luckily I fell backwards into the gutter. (*Looks at the audience for a moment.*)

Are you all following this so far?

Have you ever noticed how spring is lovely, but it fills one with sad longing because nothing in one's life will ever live up to the sweet feelings it raises, and that fall is lovely but that it fills one with sad longing because everything is dying; and life is beautiful and awful and there's no assuagement of this awful longing inside one? Have you all noticed this? I presume it's a universal feeling, isn't it? I know I feel it's universal.

(*With renewed energy.*) So, there I was lying on my back in the gutter, and this street musician came over to me and he asked me if I needed help, and I said, "No, but can you play Melancholy Baby?" And I thought that that was a pretty funny thing for me to say under the circumstances, and that I had a fair wit and intelligence even if I had been in mental institutions, and I thought to myself, maybe if this man laughs at my comment, which is wry and peculiar and yet oddly appropriate to the circumstance, that maybe I will have found a companion for the rest of my life, to help me find spring and fall less painful, summer's too hot, I wouldn't expect anyone to be able to help with that, and winter has gotten less cold than it was when I was a child, it's probably something terrible the captains of industry have done to the atmosphere, probably some ozone layer has been thinned out beyond repair, and the sun is coming through more directly, and we'll all die from it and get skin cancers, and breathe wrong things through our nostrils . . . oh God, I mustn't worry about things that may not be true and that I can't do anything about anyway. Besides which, this street musician didn't laugh at my comment about "Melancholy Baby," he looked at me very seriously and asked me if I was all right, and I said, "You don't really want to know, do you? You don't want to know how I am really, to hold me in the night, to comfort me in sickness and in health," sickness caused by the dying of the ozone layer, health caused by . . . well, who knows what causes health, probably sugar is killing all of us, and besides, I hadn't really even gotten a good look at him in the dark, maybe I wouldn't like his looks, he might not be the right person for me to spend the rest of my life with anyway. And then he asked me if I wanted help to stand up or if I wanted to stay seated in the gutter, and I thought to myself, I don't know the answer to this question. And so I said, with a laugh, "I don't know the answer to that question, ask me another one," which I thought was kind of a funny remark in the circumstances, this crazy lady in the gutter after she's attacked someone at the tuna fish counter and been assaulted by a taxi driver, sort of gallant and witty in the midst of unspeakable woe.

What is that line from Beckett? "Laughing wild amid severest woe."

So then I said to him, with another wry smile, "I am laughing wild amid severest woe." And he looked at me blankly, and I said, "I am laughing wild!" And since he didn't seem to get it, I threw back my head, and I let out this enormous, frightening laugh I do at parties: AHAHAHAHAHAHAHAHAHAHAHAH! And he looked alarmed and then he said, if you need help getting to the ladies shelter, I'll be over there playing my guitar. And then I knew I'd been fortune's fool, that this man was not meant to share my life with me, he was humorless, he didn't have a sense of shared existential ennui, angst, whatever, I've been to college. Although I didn't read everything they assigned me, of course. What good would it have done? (*Looks at the audience.*)

Do you follow me so far?

Do you feel a kinship, or are you looking at me like that street musician did?

You know, sometimes I love street musicians—not that particular one, of course, but sometimes if one is walking down the grubby street, like yesterday I was, and this young girl was playing a cello, all by herself, it was late, it was dark, the city was filled with horrible people—outpatients from Creedmoor, some of whom I know; horrible teenagers from New Jersey who come on dates pretending that life is *wonderful,* they'll learn, I hope they cry a hundred tears; I have this hostility toward anyone who is happy. But I do appreciate beauty, and the strains of melancholy comfort rising from this young woman's cello brought a momentary peace to my soul. I stood for a moment and listened in awe, and then I gave her a nickel. You may think that was cheap, but it was a nickel bag of coke. AHAHAHAHAHAHAHA!

No, I'm kidding, it was just a nickel, five cents. I only listened to it for a moment, I can't be expected to support the woman, she plays well, why doesn't she get a job in the state symphony and not be out and about on the streets, irritating everyone, making them feel guilty? No, but that contradicts the point I was making. I love street musicians. (*She sings for a bit, prettily; in New York, she sang a bit of "Vilia" from Franz Lehar's "The Merry Widow."*)*

You may ask, what parties has she gone to to unleash this peculiar laugh? Mostly the Warhol crowd. One of the orderlies at Creedmoor said to me, you remind me of Edie Sedgewick, I bet Andy Warhol would like you. This was

---

*See Special Note on copyright page.

before he died, of course. And so one of the times I wasn't institutionalized I went to a party that Warhol was at, supposedly, but I never met him. That's why I haven't had the film career Edie Sedgewick had. But I haven't minded really. I think film takes away a little bit of your soul each time you're photographed. That was the theme of Ibsen's "When We Dead Awaken," only it was about sculptors, not filmmakers. I wonder if Ibsen would have liked me. I wonder if I would have liked Ibsen. I'm glad I never met Strindberg, I probably would've married him. I have a bad instinct about these sorts of things. Although who should I marry? Alan Alda? I liked him for about five minutes, but now I think he's a pill. Have you ever noticed that after you've known someone for just a little while how intolerable you find them?

And speaking of which, who is Sally Jessy Raphael? Does anyone know? I have a television in my apartment, I don't have a bed, but I have trouble sleeping anyway, sometimes I sleep in the bathtub; and she's on at three in the morning, that is, Sally Jessy Raphael is; and in some of the promos I've seen her pose with Phil Donahue, and she runs a talk show sort of like his, so I suppose she's supposed to be a kind of female Phil Donahue. But my point is, who is she? Why does she think she's interesting, or that we should listen to her? Why does she have all this self-confidence? Why doesn't she have the humility to know she's not so special? I don't have self-confidence. I think I'm special, but I have sufficient humility to question myself, maybe I'm totally worthless. But even at my most confident, I'd never try to pass myself off as a female Phil Donahue.

Plus, of course, when you're Phil Donahue you have to have opinions on so many things. I could never be President because of this. Plus, of course, if McGovern's running mate had to drop out because of shock treatments, they'd really be able to go to town with my mental history. My mental history is something, alright. I make the Frances Farmer story look like *Laugh In.* I make *The Snake Pit* look like *The Love Bug.* I make *I Never Promised You a Rose*

Garden look like *Tie A Yellow Ribbon Round the Old Oak Tree.* I make the dawn come up like thunder. Why did I say that? (*Thinks.*)

I wonder if it's because *Tie A Yellow Ribbon Round the Old Oak Tree* was sung by Tony Orlando and Dawn, ergo "dawn like thunder," in which case my unconscious mind is really active, isn't it? . . . Useless, but active.

I had such high hopes once. AHAHAHAHAHAHAHA-HAHA! She said, throwing her head back, madly. Laughing wild amid severest woe.

But what I said about having opinions—people with opinions usually pretend they know what should be done about things. I think that's hubris. Do you all know what hubris is? That's conceit, when you think you're as good as the gods. Well, everybody in this country has hubris. I'd like to take all the unwanted children in the world who some right-to-lifer keeps from being aborted, and send them all to Mother Theresa. Let her cope with the screaming, squalling little infants; she said in some interview that people who didn't want their children should send them to her rather than have an abortion. I'd like to see her dealing with three thousand shrieking infants yelling nonstop for days on end, then I hope she'd be sorry for saying such a goody-goody, disgusting thing.

I wish I had been killed when I was a fetus. It wasn't legal then, and my mother didn't think of it, but I think she'd prefer I'd never been born. I know I'd prefer she'd never have been born, and that would have taken care of my not being born as well. Plus, I'm really sick of Mother Theresa, aren't you? I mean, what makes her such a saint? She's just like Sally Jessy Raphael, only different. Oh, God, I'm starting to ramble. But I can't help it. And what does the A.A. prayer say? God help me to accept the things I cannot change. I can't change my rambling. Plus I'm not an alcoholic anyway; I just went there because I didn't know what else to do with my life, and I thought if I told them all I was an alcoholic they'd accept me. But it didn't help. They say if you don't believe in God, you just have to believe in a Higher Power than yourself, but that didn't help me particularly. I mean, who? Phil Donahue? Mother Theresa? The god Dionysus? And there was this woman at A.A. who came and said she had stopped drinking but her life hadn't been working out anyway, and how her parents were alcoholics too, and she seemed very intense and kind of crazy, and it was hard to look at her because she was missing a tooth right in front, it didn't make for an attractive package at all; and she talked about how the program had helped her realize she was powerless over alcohol, and this seemed to make her happy for some reason or other, although I think I'm powerless over lots of things and it doesn't make me happy; and then I shouted out real loud at the top of my lungs: WHY DON'T YOU GET YOUR TOOTH FIXED? And everyone looked at me real angry, and I looked embarrassed, and then I shouted: JUST A SUGGESTION. And everyone looked uncomfortable, and there was silence for about half an hour, and then the meeting was over, though we all said the A.A. prayer again; and then nobody would speak to me. But lots of people went to speak to the woman without the tooth, sort of like to prove that they didn't care she was missing her tooth; but then this one person came over to me, and said not to drink the punch, and he said that he agreed with me and that the woman looked awful; and that furthermore he'd been going to meetings for a long time, and that this woman had been missing her tooth for several years, and clearly had not organized herself into fixing this, and so he agreed with me wholeheartedly. And then he and I went to a hotel room and fucked, and then I tried to jump out the window, and then I went to Creedmoor for the third time. (*Looks thoughtful.*)

Have you all wondered why sexual intercourse sometimes makes you want to commit suicide? That is a universal feeling, isn't it? Or is it just me? Can I see a show of hands?

Oh, well, don't worry, I'm not one of those people who force audience participation. I'm not going to stand up here and insist you sing "Those Were the Days" and then when I've bullied you into it, complain you didn't sing loud enough, and then make you sing again. I've seen Pearl Bailey and Diana Ross do that, it's really obnoxious. I want to see them killed.

Tell me, are you enjoying my company, or are you wishing I'd go away? I can never tell in life, it's one of my problems. Reality testing of any sort is a mystery to me, my doctors say. I have the most wonderful doctors, they're all like Dr. Ruth Westheimer on television. Have you seen how she's listed in the TV Guide? It says, *Good Sex,* dash, Dr. Ruth Westheimer. And they wonder why I have reality testing problems. What could that mean on television, I wonder. Andy Warhol said everyone would be famous for fifteen minutes in the twentieth century, but she's already been famous for far longer than that, it doesn't look like she's ever going to go away. Eventually we'll see her on *Password* where no matter what word she's trying to communicate, she'll only talk sex. Say, the word is "nicotine." Her first clue will be "clitoris." Then "stimulation." Then "cunnilingus." Her partner will be totally baffled, especially when the host says, "No, Marjorie, I'm sorry, the word was nicotine." Then Dr. Ruth will laugh like crazy, just like me. AHAHAHAHAHAHAHAHA!

(*Suddenly angry, and for real.*) But her partner will have lost the game thanks to her stupid clues. She won't receive the seven hundred dollars for the first round, she will not win the trip for two to the Caribbean, to stay at the luxurious Hyatt Regency, she will not get to move on to the Speed Round where she could win thirty thousand dollars if she can guess eight words in thirty seconds, all because this nutty, smutty doctor thinks she's cute, and thinks she knows something about something, and has hubris like every other fucking creature in this stupid, horrible universe. *I want Dr. Ruth Westheimer and Mother Theresa to fight to the death in the colliseum!!!*— using knives and swords and heavy metal balls with spikes on them! And then when one of them has her sword to the other one's throat, I want to raise my hand and give the "thumbs down" sign just like Siskel and Ebert dismissing a particularly dreadful movie; and then I want Ronald Reagan hung upside down over sulphur emissions and made to inhale toxic waste, just like those animals who are made to smoke three million cigarettes; and then I want Mayor Koch made to *eat* Westway; and then I want the world to come to a complete and total end, ka-plooey, ka-ploppy, ka-plopp! AHAHAHAHA-HAHAHAHAHAHAHAHAHAHA!

Do you get how I feel? Do you identify in some way, or are you rejecting me? Would any of you give me a job ever? I can't believe you would.

Because I have tried to improve my life, I have fought, I have called people on the phone and screamed at them, "LET ME BABYSIT WITH YOUR CHILDREN, I PROMISE I WON'T KILL THEM," but then they don't hire me. I've called editors at Doubleday and Knopf and St. Martin's Press even, and I've said to them over the telephone, "I DON'T KNOW HOW TO TYPE AND I'M TOO UNSTABLE TO READ, BUT IF YOU HIRE ME TO BE AN ASSISTANT EDITOR I COULD TRY TO BE MORE STABLE, HUH, WHADDYA SAY?"

But do they hire me ever? What do you think? No? If you think no, raise your hand. I want to see how many of you think no. I WANT SOME AUDIENCE PARTICIPATION HERE, RAISE YOUR GODDAM HANDS! That's better. And that's right, the answer is no. Now I want everyone to hold hands and sing "Give peace a chance." No, I'm kidding, I said I hated audience participation and so I do.

The word is flashlight. Dr. Ruth's clues are: Clitoris. Erect nipple. Mound of Venus. Pound of penis. AHAHA-HAHAHA, I didn't know I was going to say that.

But, Dr. Ruth, I can't get the word "flashlight" from those clues. You're not helping me to win the prize. I can't get the prize with those clues. (*Starts to cry.*) I can't get the prize with those clooooooooeeess. Oh God, I want to die, I want to die. (*Cries violently. Silence for a bit; her crying subsides.*)

Uh, it's quite a relief having me silent for a while, isn't it? (*Smiles or laughs a bit, and continues to be silent.*)

My favorite book is *Bleak House.* Not the book, but the title. I haven't read the book. I've read the title. The title sounds the way I feel. And my most recent accomplishment was getting up out of the gutter after I fell down leaving that crazy taxi driver. And my Scotch is Dewar's White Label.

I feel terribly sorry for my doctors. My doctors get exhausted listening to me, I can tell they feel my words are charging out of my mouth and trying to invade their brain cells, and they're frightened. Understandably. And that's why I try to practice being quiet from time to time. Let me be quiet for a second again. (*She is quiet.*)

You see, you need that rest too, don't you?

Here is the key to existence. Are you all listening? Here is the key to existence; when I tell you this you will know how to run your lives. You will know if you have been living life to the full, and if you realize you haven't been, you will know immediately how to correct that state of affairs. As soon as I tell you the key to existence. Are you ready? Are you ready for me to tell you?

Oh, dear, I've built it up too much, and it's really not all that significant. But it's what I got from the est training: *Always breathe.* That's the basis of life, breathing. That's basically the basis. If you don't breathe, you die. (*Pause.*)

Well, it seemed more impressive when you hadn't slept

for two days. If you're rested, it doesn't sound so important, but I try to hold on to it.

The other major thing I have learned is . . . (*Sincerely.*) well, I've forgotten it, so it couldn't have been too significant.

Let me try to summarize what I've told you, and then I'll remove myself from your presence. I had trouble buying tuna fish, then I had an argument with a taxi driver, I fell in the gutter, I like street musicians sometimes, I have a startling laugh, Ahahahahaha, I don't like Sally Jessy Raphael, Mother Theresa or Dr. Ruth Westheimer, I am opposed to "hubris," I wish I had never been born, I have trouble getting a job, I haven't read *Bleak House* but I like the title, and I have learned that you should always breathe.

Oh, and I feel great hostility toward teenagers from New Jersey who seem happy. I mentioned that earlier, didn't I? I think I did.

Well, then, I've covered everything I intended to. Thank you for giving me your attention. Goodbye, I love you. Of course, that's a lie. Some of you I think are first class fools, and I hate you. In fact, I probably don't like any of you. Curse you! I curse all of you! May your children have webbed feet, and all your house pets get mange and worms! AHAHAHAHAHA!

I'm terribly sorry. I really can't leave you that way. The management would be so cranky if I cursed the audience right at the end of my speech, so forget I said that. I do love you. M-wah! I want to be a responsible member of this society, so give me a job if you can, I'm sure I can do *some*thing. I love you, m-wah! The ushers will give you my phone number, and the box office will field any job offers you call in. Thank you. Goodbye. Goodbye. I hope your lives are better than mine. Laugh laugh laugh laugh—I'm getting too tired to do the real laugh right now. Laugh

laugh laugh. Laughing is a tonic. So forget crying. Cry, and you cry alone. Laugh and you . . . cry alone later.

And remember—always breathe. Even if I stop, you keep breathing out there, alright? Keep breathing. In and out. In and out. In and out. (*She breathes in and out several times in a somewhat exaggerated manner, as if to show us how. She then stops the exaggerated breathing, and looks at us for a few beats. She's either holding her breath or, more likely, just breathing regularly, as the lights dim.*)

2. SEEKING WILD

Scene

A space in which a talk is about to be given. It could be a lecture hall, a stage, a room, a "space."

In the New York production there was a dark curtain mid-stage. In front of the curtain R. *was a chair next to a table. On the table were a water pitcher and a glass.*

On L. *was a column-like stand (a pedestal), on which were three crystals: a large, jagged clear crystal; a chunk of amethyst (which is purple); a piece of citrine (amber-colored).*

Hanging on the curtain, Upstage Center, and rather dominating the stage was a very large hand-painted canvas poster of an Egyptian Eye. The New York poster was patterned after the Eye of Ra (or "Horus card") found in the book The Way of Cartouche.

Whatever it's based on, it should be a large eye, not realistically drawn but with a primitive, bold look to it. Beneath the eye there is a small line (sort of where "circles under your eyes" would be) off of which hang little icicles or tear drops or some such design. Again, whatever "hangs" beneath the eye should not look realistically like anything; it should be some bold, primitive design one can't quite figure out.

This Egyptian Eye poster should look mysterious, otherworldly, and should give a sense that the talk the audience is about to hear may be "mind-expanding," Jungian, New Age-related, etc. etc.

After a few beats, a Man enters. (He might briefly look at the "Eye" poster, and register slight confusion.)

The Man is dressed well, maybe even a little trendy. He is dressed up to give a talk, to share his new thoughts.

He carries with him a few file cards that he has made notes on. He smiles at the audience briefly, checks his first note card quickly before beginning, and then speaks with earnestness and purpose.

MAN. I used to be a very negative person. But then I took this personality workshop that totally turned my life around. Now when something bad or negative happens, I can see the positive. Now when I have a really bad day or when someone I thought was a really good friend betrays me, or maybe when I've been hit by one of those damn people riding bicycles the opposite way on a one-way street, so, of course, one hadn't looked in that direction and there they are bearing down on you, about to kill or maim you — anyway, I look at any of these things and I say to myself: this glass is not half full, it's half empty.

No — I said it backwards, force of habit. This glass is not half empty, it is half *full*.

Of course, if they hit you with the stupid bicycle your glass will not be half full or half empty, it will be shattered to pieces, and you'll be dead or in the hospital.

But really I'm trying to be positive, that's what I'm doing with my life these days.

(*Reads from a note card.*) I was tired of not being joyful and happy, I was sick of my personality, and I had to change it.

(*Off the card; back to speaking extemporaneously.*) Half full, *not* half empty. I had to say to myself: you do not have cancer—at least not today. You are not blind. You are not one of the starving children in India or China or in Africa. Look at the sunset, look at the sunrise, why don't you enjoy them, for God's sake? And now I do. (*Almost as a sidetrack to himself.*) Except if it's cloudy, of course, and you can't see the sun. Or if it's cold. Or if it's too hot.

(*Hearing his negativity above.*) I probably need to take a few more personality workshops to complete the process. It's still not quite within my grasp, this being positive business.

(*Reads from cards again.*) But I'm making great strides. My friends don't recognize me. (*Smiles.*)

(*Off the cards again.*) And it is hard for me to be positive because I'm very sensitive to the vibrations of people around me, or maybe I'm just paranoid. But in any case, I used to find it difficult to go out of the house sometimes because of coming into contact with other people.

You've probably experienced something similar—you know, the tough on the subway who keeps staring at you and you're the only two people in the car and he keeps staring and after a while you think, does he want to kill me? Or just intimidate me? Which is annoying enough.

Or the people in movie theatres who talk endlessly during the opening credits so you can just *tell* they're going to talk through the entire movie and that it will be utterly useless to ask them not to talk.

And even if you do ask them not to talk and they ungraciously acquiesce, they're going to send out vibrations that they hate you all during the entire film, and then it will be impossible to concentrate.

You can move, but the person next to you in the new location will probably, you know, rattle candy wrappers endlessly all through the movie. Basically I don't go to the movies anymore. What's the point?

But even if you can skip going to the movies, you pretty much have to go to the supermarket.

(*Steps closer to the audience.*) I was in the supermarket the other day about to buy some tuna fish when I sensed this very disturbed presence right behind me. There was something about her focus that made it very clear to me that she was a disturbed person. So I thought—well, you should never look at a crazy person directly, so I thought, I'll just keep looking at these tuna fish cans, pretending to be engrossed in whether they're in oil or in water, and the person will then go away. But instead *wham!* she brings her fist down on my head and screams "would you move, asshole"! (*Pause.*)

Now why did she do that? She hadn't even said, "would you please move" at some initial point, so I would've known what her problem was. Admittedly I don't always tell people what I want either—like the people in the movie theatres who keep talking, you know, I just give up and resent them—but on the other hand, I don't take my fist and go wham! on their heads!

I mean, analyzing it, looking at it in a positive light, this woman probably had some really horrible life story that, you know, kind of, explained how she got to this point in time, hitting me in the supermarket. And perhaps if her life—*since birth*—had been explained to me, I could probably have made some sense out of her action and how she got there. But even with that knowledge—which I didn't have—it was *my* head she was hitting, and it's just so unfair.

It makes me want to never leave my apartment *ever ever again.* (*Suddenly he closes his eyes and moves his arms in a circular motion around himself, round and round, soothingly.*)

I am the predominant source of energy in my life. I let go of the pain from the past. I let go of the pain from the present. In the places in my body where pain lived previously, now there is light and love and joy. (*He opens his eyes again and looks at the audience peacefully and happily.*)

That was an affirmation.

Now the theory of affirmations is that by saying something positive about yourself in the present tense—as if the positive thing is already happening—you draw in positive energies to you. For instance, who do you think will have the easier life?—someone who goes around saying inside their head, "Everyone hates me, they try to avoid me, my job stinks, my life is miserable." Or the person who says "Everyone likes me exactly as I am, every time I turn around people offer me friendship and money, my life is delightful and effortless." (*Pause.*)

Obviously, the second person will be much happier.

There's an additional theory that by thinking negatively, you actually cause, and are thus responsible for, the bad things that happen to you. Thus I need to look at whether I maybe *caused* the woman in the tuna fish aisle to hit me on the head. Or, since that sounds rather blaming, I need to look at the incident and see how else I could have behaved so she might *not* have hit me on the head.

When I sensed her presence, rather than doing nothing and pretending I didn't *notice* that she seemed odd, maybe I could have said, "Is something the matter?" Then maybe she would have said, yes, you're in my way, and I would have moved. Or, if when I said "Is something the matter?", she stayed hostile and said "why???" defensively or something, if I stayed honest and said . . . "well, you seem odd." Or "I sense you're distressed," she might have felt that I was "responding" to her as another human being, and that might have relaxed her, and *then* she might have told me what was the matter.

So you see, I shouldn't feel like a victim. We have power.

(*Reads from his notecards.*) We can change our own thoughts, from negative to positive. (*Off the cards again; explaining.*) Say I feel bad; I can *choose* to feel good.

How do I feel right now? (*Thinks.*) I feel fine. Everything's fine. Of course, that's just on the surface, underneath there's always this gnawing residue of anxiety. But is feeling anxious just part of the human condition? Or do I feel more anxious than one should normally due to some psychological maladjustment or something? Maybe I wasn't breast-fed enough as an infant. Actually I don't even know if I was breast-fed at all. (*Thinks with concern about his lack of knowledge concerning this.*) Oh well, enough about breast feeding.

(*A surge of positive energy:*) Let me try to *change* how I feel. Let me try to feel happy for a moment. (*Closes his eyes, puts his fingers to his forehead and "flicks away" negative energy; waits for happiness.*)

No, I was just thinking about Chernobyl. That's like a scream from the universe warning us, but we're not paying attention. I can't believe they don't know what to do with nuclear waste, and then they keep building these things. I'm sorry, I was trying to feel happy. Let me try again. (*Closes his eyes, tries again.*)

Sorry, I was just thinking of something else, something I read in the newspaper about this fourteen-year-old boy in Montana who shot his geometry teacher—*to death*—

because the teacher was flunking him. Now that's crazy enough—but it seems that this particular teacher didn't come to school that day, and so this fourteen-year-old boy shot the substitute teacher instead. Shot her dead. I don't know how to cope with that.

I mean, positive thinking aside, how do you protect yourself from these sorts of things? (*Suddenly wants some water, goes up to table and pours himself some while he's on this tangent of upset and negativity.*)

And there's acid rain and something wrong with the ozone layer, and the Secretary of Education doesn't want schools to educate students about the dangers of nuclear proliferation, but instead to focus on how terrible the communists are. And the Secretary of the Environment isn't in favor of protecting the environment, doesn't see a problem. The appointments of these offices in the Reagan administration seem like a sick joke . . . like naming Typhoid Mary the Secretary of Health and Welfare. God, it's discouraging. (*Drinks water.*)

And think about God. You know, it was nice to believe in God, and an afterlife; and I'm sometimes envious of the people who seem comfortable because they still have this belief. But I remember when everybody won Tonys for *Dreamgirls,* and they all got up there thanking God for letting them win this award, and I was thinking to myself: God is silent on the holocaust, but He involves himself in the Tony awards? It doesn't seem very likely. (*Feels a need for affirmation; does the circular arm motions again.*)

I am the predominant source of my life. I release anger from my solar plexus. It is replaced by serenity and white light and joy and . . . serenity. Everything in my life works. Except the plumbing, and career and relationships. (*Laughs at his joke, then talks sincerely.*)

I'm sorry, I was planning on being positive out here, and

it's just not happening. But I guess whatever happens is ok. Is that right?

This personality workshop I took taught me that I judge things too much, that some things just "are," you don't have to label them. And also that you shouldn't judge feelings.

This workshop also said to forgive yourself for what you haven't achieved. For instance, I had wanted to be a university professor, maybe in New England somewhere—summers off, tutorials, sherry. I'm very verbal, and that would have been a good thing to do with it.

Instead I work for a magazine, not a bad job, but not great—it's sort of a cross between . . . *TV Guide* and pornography. Well, that's too strong—but I do have to interview people who are on television series, and if they're at all attractive, they have them photographed with their blouses undone or with their shirts off. Sometimes I have nightmares about the upper bodies of Barbara Bach and Lorenzo Lamas. People whose first and last names begin with the same letter. Lorenzo Lamas. Erik Estrada. Suzanne Sommers. Cher. (*Time for another affirmation.*)

Everything unfolds in my life exactly as it should, including my career. Abundance is my natural state of being, and I accept it now. I let go of anger and resentment. (*A sudden addition to the affirmation.*) I love the woman in the tuna fish aisle. I accept her exactly as she is. I accept myself exactly as I am. I approve of my body. (*Makes equivocal face.*) I approve of *other* people's bodies.

You know, I don't like meeting people who are too attractive, and not just TV stars at my job, but anyone who's good-looking or charismatic. I hate being attracted to people, it's exhausting. It stirs up longing.

Of course, one can just do one's best to have sex with the

person, and that assuages some of the longing. But the problem is, that sexual longing has no real assuagement ever, it's like longing for the moon; you can never have the moon no matter what you do, and if you were foolish enough to take a spaceship up there—and if the people running NASA didn't see to it that you were killed—you would just find that the moon was this big chunk of nothing that had nothing to do with what you were longing for at all. Oh, Olga, let's go to Moscow, and all that. There is no Moscow, there is no moon, there is no assuagement of longing.

(*Affirmation.*) I let go of my need for longing. I let go of sexual interest. I become like Buddha, and want nothing. (*Abruptly stops; to audience.*) Do these affirmations sound right to you? They sound off to me.

And I've certainly never successfully acted them out. Cause as soon as sexual attraction kicks in, the zen in one's nature flies out the window. You meet someone, sometimes they really are terrific, other times they're just awful but nonetheless you find yourself attracted to them anyway, knowing you're an utter fool and will be very sorry later on. And then the pursuit begins. All those opening weeks of interested conversation, with the eyes more lively than usual, and each party finding the other's comments and insights more than usually charming and delightful. And then if you've been in therapy like me, there are the flirtatious exchanges of childhood traumas—all of my family were borderline schizophrenic, they beat me, they had terrible taste in furniture—and after a while one's mind starts to reverberate with, when will I have an orgasm with this person?

If there is a God, his design about sex is certainly humiliating. It's humiliating to want things. And sex itself people say is beautiful—but is it? Maybe you think it is. Terrible viscous discharges erupting in various openings may strike you as the equivalent of the Sistine Chapel ceiling, for all I know. It doesn't strike me that way. (*He stops. He realizes how extreme and crank-like his comments have begun to sound. He smiles at the audience, wanting to re-establish his rapport with them, and his reasonability.*)

But I am being negative again. And clearly sex isn't just disgusting. I know that, and you know that. And when I'm lucky enough to go off with someone to his or her apartment, I certainly anticipate a pleasant time. (*Now he stops dead. He had no intention of going into this area of his life with this audience, and he's suddenly uncertain how he even got into it. Or, more to the point, how he can get out of it. He thinks, can't come up with any way to camouflage or take back what he's just said. For better or for worse, he decides just to speak honestly.*)

As the "his or her" comment suggests, I am attracted to women and to men. Though more frequently to other guys, which I find rather embarrassing to admit to publicly. Why do I bring it *up* publicly then, you may well ask? Well . . . I don't know. Why not? All my relatives are dead, and those that aren't I'm willing not to talk to.

And things like the recent Supreme Court ruling that sex between consenting adult homosexuals *not* be included in what's considered the rights of privacy—this makes me think it's now important to be open about this. Look, I've even brought pictures of myself in bed with people! (Pats his inside jacket pocket.) At intermission the ushers will let you look at them! . . . although I suppose the Meese Commission will run in here and try to take them away from you and then force you to buy milk at a 7-11 store. God, I took some Valium before I came out here, but it hasn't calmed me down a bit.

Anyway, I didn't mean to get into this . . . (*Puts his notecards away in his jacket.*) . . . but I find the Supreme Court's ruling on this issue deeply disturbing. I mean, so much of the evil that men do to one another has at its core the inability of people to *empathize* with another person's position. Say when you're seven, you find yourself slightly more drawn to Johnny than you are to Jane. This is not a conscious decision on your part, it just happens, it's an instinct like . . . liking the color blue.

Now in less tolerant times, you were put to death for this attraction. As time went on, this punishment was sometimes reduced to mere castration, or just imprisonment. Until recently this attraction was considered so horrific that society pretty much expected you to lie to yourself about your sexual and emotional feelings, and if you couldn't do that, certainly expected you to *shut* up about it, and go live your life bottled up and terrified; and if you would be so kind as to never have any physical closeness with anyone *ever,* when you were buried you could know that society would feel you had handled your disgraceful situation with tact and will power. That was one *cheery* option—nothing, and then the grave.

Or, you might make a false marriage with some woman who wouldn't know what was going on with you, and you could *both* be miserable and unfulfilled. That was *another* respectable option. Or you might kill yourself. There's not a lot of empathy evident in the people who prefer these options. (*He takes out his notecards again, starts to look at them, but then his mind isn't ready to leave this topic yet.*)

I mean, *I* certainly realize how insane it would be to ask a heterosexual to deny his or her natural sexual feelings and perform homosexual acts that went against *their* nature. If I can have that empathy, why can't others have the same empathy in reverse? I want some empathy here! (*Goes into an affirmation.*) I am the predominant source of . . . well, fuck that. (*Throws his notecards over his shoulder, drives on ahead.*)

And then, of course, there are all the religious teachings about homosexuality. The Book of Leviticus, for instance, says that homosexuals should basically be put to death. It also tells you how to sacrifice rams and bullocks, and instructs you not to sit in a chair sat in by any woman who's had her period in the last seven days or something. To me, this is not a book to look to for much modern wisdom. (*If the audience laughs, he might smile with them.*)

People's concepts of God are so odd. For instance, take the Christians—"take them, please"—who seem to believe that God is so disgusted by the sexual activities of homosexuals that He created AIDS to punish them, apparently waiting until 1978 or so to do this, even though homosexual acts have been going on for considerably longer than that, at least since . . . 1956.

I mean, what do they think? God sits around in a lounge chair chatting with Gabriel, planning the fall foliage in Vermont—"I think a lot of orange this year"—when suddenly he says: Boy oh boy do I find homosexuals disgusting. I'm going to give them a really horrifying disease!

And Gabriel says: Oh yes?

[God] Yes! And drug addicts and . . . and . . . hemophiliacs! (*Gabriel looks fairly appalled.*)

[Gabriel] But why hemophiliacs?

[God] Oh, no reason. I want the disease to go through the bloodstream and even though I'm all powerful and can do everything cause I'm God, I'm too tired today to figure out how to connect the disease to the bloodstream and *not* affect hemophiliacs. Besides, the suffering will be good for them.

[Gabriel] Really? In what way?

[God] Oh, I don't know. I'll explain it at the end of the world.

[Gabriel] I see. Tell me, what about the children of drug addicts? Will they get the disease through their mother's wombs?

[God] Oh, I hadn't thought about that. Well—why not? Serve the hophead mothers right. Boy oh boy, do I hate women drug addicts!

[Gabriel] Yes, but why punish their babies?

[God] And I hate homosexuals!

[Gabriel] Yes, yes, we got you hate homosexuals . . .

[God] Except for Noel Coward, he was droll.

[Gabriel] Yes, he was droll.

[God] And I hate Haitians. Anything beginning with the letter "h."

[Gabriel] Yes, but isn't it unfair to infect innocent babies in the womb with this dreadful disease?

[God] Look, homosexuals and drug addicts are very, very bad people; and if babies get it, well, don't forget I'm God, so you better just presume I have some secret reason why it's good they get it too.

[Gabriel] Yes, but what *is* this secret reason?

[God] Stop asking so many questions.

[Gabriel] Yes, but . . .

[God] There you go again, trying to horn in on the Tree of Knowledge just like Adam and Eve did. Boy oh boy does that make me wrathful. Okay, Gabriel, you asked for it: I hereby sentence you to become man; I give you suffering and death; I give you psychological pain; I give you AIDS, your immune system will shut down totally, you'll die from brain tumors and diarrhea, and horrible random infections. I give you bone cancer, lymph cancer, breast cancer —lots of cancer.

(*A good idea, whimsical.*) Oh! . . . and I hereby revoke penicillin. Anyone out there who has ever been exposed to sypyhilis will suffer and die just like they used to — as a side issue, I love to connect sex and death, I don't know why I invented sex to begin with, it's a revolting idea, but as long as I have, I want it done *properly* in the *missionary* position with *one* person for life, or I want those who disobey me to die a horrible death from AIDS and syphilis and God knows what else. Is that clear???

(*Breaks "character," talks to the audience as himself again.*) Now surely that God can't exist — I mean, surely the Christ who said "Blessed are the merciful" could hardly have come from such a raging, spiteful God. (*Pause, his agitation not quite gone yet. He turns around and stares* U. *at the "Egyptian Eye" banner for a moment. Turns back to the audience.*)

What *is* that??? (*Looks again. Then back.*)

You know, I don't want to take *away* faith in God from anyone who has it; it's just that I don't follow it. And it's not as if living without a belief in God is so pleasant. In moments of deep despair you have absolutely nothing to fall back on. You just stay in the deep despair for a while, and then if you're lucky, you go to sleep.

But I find more and more that I'm starting to long for some sense of value in things. My mind wanders to reincarnation and karma and karmic paths and so on; in some ways I am turning into Shirley MacLaine. Now one does laugh at her, but I'm starting to really identify with the desire to find some meaning out there.

Because I'm really tired of where I've been. I've been . . . a pretty good "ad-hoc existentialist" for about twenty years. I've gotten up every morning, and I've carried on with my life, acting decent and getting things done, while all the time believing none of it mattered. And I'm really sick of it. I'm *starved* for some meaning. For some belief in something. I'm tired of being an existentialist. It's hard to be joyful when you're an existentialist. Albert Camus was not a laugh riot.

I even went to the Harmonic Convergence ceremony in Central Park this summer. Do you know what I'm referring to? It's this strange, New Age-connected belief, prophesied in several ancient cultures—the Mayan, the Aztec, Hopi Indians—that August 16th and 17th of 1987 represent a window in time in which the planets line up in some special way or other, and that, supposedly, there is an opportunity for mankind to make a spiritual shift away from pollution and destruction of the planet back to being "in alignment" with mother earth, and so on.

The newspapers made fun of the event, and people at the magazine where I work thought I was nuts; but I found I really wanted to believe in this Harmonic Convergence. And even if it were a lot of nonsense, I *liked* the idea of people getting up in the morning all over the world to greet the sunrise and to, if nothing else, sort of hope for a better way of living. I mean, it beats a punch in the eye, doesn't it?

So a couple of friends and I—I'm starting to have more friends who think this way—set our alarms for four in the morning to head up to 83rd and Central Park West, which had been designated as a sacred site. (*Realizing that sounds a bit funny.*) Or at least as a place where people were going to gather.

We went over to 6th Avenue for a taxi and saw all these people getting out of cabs who looked like they were leaving clubs together, going home to have sex, or take cocaine or . . . otherwise give *New York* magazine topics to write on. I guess people still go to clubs. I don't really know anyone who does.

Anyway, predictably we got an absolutely *terrifying* taxi driver. He'd race up to every red light at sixty miles an hour, never slowing down at all just in case the light turned green, which it sometimes did, but you had to worry about the people coming in the other direction who might be trying to run their lights. Anyway, it was harrowing. I kept saying to myself, "All is well in my universe, everyone is calm, no one rushes;" but it didn't make him slow down. Finally I had to say, slow down, goddam it, only I didn't say goddam it, and he didn't slow down, and eventually we killed two people and a dog. Well, just kidding. But it was a disorienting beginning to the Harmonic Convergence.

Well, in any case, at the sacred site itself, it was very crowded, and there was incense and so on, and wind chimes, and we all sat in a circle. And in the center of the circle there were five women and one man who were blowing on conch shells; and one of the women explained to the crowd that we were all there to align the "horizontal plane" of our present existence with the "vertical plane" of mother earth and the planets or . . . something like that . . . but she seemed a very *warm* woman—she reminded me of someone I know and like named Martha Rhodes. And then the woman said we should all join in and makes sounds like the conch shell if we wanted to, and eventually most of the crowd sort of hit this one sustained note that in these circles is described as "toning." (*He takes a moment to breathe and then lets out a low, sustained note, kind of like chanting "ohm." It's just a held note.*) Ahhhhhhhhhhhhhhhhhhhhhhhhhhhhhhhhhhhmmmmm mmmmmmmmmmmm.

I liked doing that. I'm not comfortable meditating yet, but this I could do, and it was nice to be connected to the crowd that way.

And then the sun came up, but the "sacred site chosen" had all these *trees* around it so you couldn't actually *see* the sun. I had almost gone to my friend's roof and part of me wished I were there instead. And then this sort of . . . loopy woman who'd been dancing around the periphery of the circle saying kind of corny things like "I dance for mother moon and sister star" and stuff like that; and whom I almost admired for having the guts to say things like that, and yet I also thought her sensibility was kind of . . . icky . . . anyway, she got up and invited everyone who wanted to, to get up and share their hopes and dreams and prayers for the future. And I realized I didn't want to hear *everyone* in the crowd verbalize their hopes, we'd be stuck for *hours,* listening to a lot of gobbledegook.

And then, of course, the first person to get up to share with the group was one of those mental patients who wander the streets of New York—she looked *demented,* and she was yellow from nicotine, and she talked on and on. And what she said wasn't wrong, exactly—something about why don't people say "I love you" rather than "I hate you"?—but it was upsetting that she was crazy—she reminded me of the woman in the tuna fish aisle, but much more clearly crazy, the woman in the tuna fish aisle could pass for normal on a good day, but this woman really couldn't.

And then the "icky woman" gave the "demented woman" a great big hug in order to *shut her up,* and then some teenager got up to recite a song—not sing it, *recite* it. I don't remember what song it was. Maybe "Blowin' in the Wind." (*Jokes.*) Or "Bali Ha'i." Anyway, it was turning into a nightmare. I didn't want anyone else to speak, I just wanted instant transformation of the planet, and I didn't want to take potluck of listening to any strangers in the crowd say how we should go about it, I didn't trust that they'd know, I just *wanted the transformation.* I didn't want to have to deal with *people* about it. And the Harmonic Convergence is about people coming together, and here I was disliking everyone. So I wasn't being very transformed. And my back was sore from sitting—I need to exercise, but I guess I never will, so I asked my friends if we could *please* leave the group and go out into an open area of the park so that we could actually see the sun.

And we did that, and the Great Lawn was very pretty,

but I was irritated that we hadn't been there for the actual sunrise.

Well, you can see I was quite resistant; and I did feel bad I was judging everyone there, but then it doesn't really work to pretend you're not feeling something you're feeling. But when you're judging people, you certainly don't feel a sense of unity, do you?

Maybe I shouldn't be so judgmental of people. And it was moving that everyone went there and showed up. I liked that part. And I liked the toning. But otherwise, I felt . . . very separate. (*He looks thoughtful and a little sad at this. He stays in the moment for a bit, and then goes into another affirmation, moving his arms in that circular motion again.*)

I am *not* separate. I am one with the universe. We are all one. We are all part of the same divine energy. (*His tone becomes slightly tongue-in-cheek.*) There are spirit guides above, waiting to guide us. They speak to us through Shirley MacLaine; they knew enough not to choose Shelley Winters. These spirit guides help us. They drive Shirley's car, they make airline reservations for her, they're just great. Bali Ha'i will call you, any night, any day. And they call the wind Maria.* Kumbaya, kumbayae.**

Well, now I've depressed myself. But I really am much more positive than I ever used to be; and I think these affirmations are a good thing. It's just that . . . sometimes the bottom drops out for me. And then I need to go sleep for a while, and see if tomorrow feels better.

(*Looks around at banner again.*) I wish I knew what that was. It's a great big eye, I see that. I don't know what those things dripping off it are. It looks Egyptian. Or Columbus Avenue. I shouldn't make fun of it. Maybe it is a guide.

---

*pronounced Ma-rye-a

**Kumbayae rhymes with day

(*Makes something up.*) It's an "all-seeing eye" that represents inner knowingness, all the wisdom we know from the collective unconscious but, alas, have forgotten. (*He looks over to the crystals, and crosses to them.*)

What about crystals? Do you think crystals work? *What works,* do you think? (*He stares at the crystals, wondering what works.*)

Let me try to feel happy again. (*Puts his fingers to his forehead, "flicks" away negativity; pause.*) Let me hold a crystal to my head and try to feel happy. (*Holds the clear crystal to his head; pause; puts the crystal down again.*) Let me give up on feeling happy for now, and just concentrate on breathing. (*He takes an intake of breath, but stops and comes closer to the audience, a little disappointed.*) I don't feel I've helped you very much. But I want you to remember what I said about affirmations. We *can* change our thoughts. And even when we can't, just kinda . . . try to . . . *silence your mind,* and then just breathe. As the last thing between us, let's just breathe, alright? (*He breathes in an exaggerated way, so the audience can get in synch with him. On the intake of breath he moves his arms up from his diaphragm to his chin; on the outtake, his arms relax downward, the palms open in the "receiving" mode. He keeps his eyes closed.*) In, out. In, out. In, out. God, life's monotonous, isn't it? No, I keep judging things, I'm going to stop doing that. I'm going to stop talking. Just breathe. (*He returns to his exaggerated breathing again, this time without words. Intake—arms up to chin; outtake—arms down to the side. He keeps his eyes closed, except on his second full breath when he opens them to check how the audience is doing, breathing with him. On his third breath, he closes his eyes again, and the lights fade.*)

3. DREAMING WILD

Scene 1

The tuna fish counter in a supermarket.

The Man is staring at tuna fish cans, deciding which one to buy.

The Woman comes and stands behind him, waiting for him to get out of her way. Her energy is odd, and she is already overly impatient.

He senses her odd energy, kind of half looks behind him; then decides not to meet her eye—you shouldn't look at a crazy person—and he starts studying one particular tuna fish can with intensity, hoping she will soon go away.

After a few moments this becomes intolerable for the Woman and she raises up her fist and brings it down on the Man's head. The Man is so thrown off-balance that he falls to the ground.

WOMAN. Would you kindly move, *asshole*! (*From off* R., *the sound of a child crying, as if startled by the Woman's ferocity.*)
MAN. What's the matter with you????
WOMAN. Why didn't you move? I asked you to move!
MAN. No, you didn't!
WOMAN. Yes, I did! (*To off-stage, where the crying is coming from.*) Stop crying, little girl, I didn't do anything!
MAN. You're crazy! (*The Woman herself starts to cry, and she runs out of the supermarket. The Man stares after her, rubbing his head.*)

BLACKOUT

SCENE 2

Lights up again on the supermarket aisle.

The Man is once again looking at tuna.

The Woman once again comes in, and stands behind him.

The audience should see that we are replaying the same scene again, so the Man and Woman's actions should be pretty close to what they did in the previous brief scene.

The Woman's energy is odd, and she is already overly impatient.

He senses her odd energy, decides not to meet her eye, and starts studying one particular tuna fish can with intensity, hoping she will soon go away.

The Woman suddenly speaks with suppressed fury.

WOMAN. (*Angry, through clenched teeth so it's hard to understand her.*) You reading a book? I don't have the *time*!
MAN. (*Confused; looks at his watch.*) Um . . . it's about 6:30.
WOMAN. That's not what I said, *asshole*! (*Woman hits him on the top of the head, He falls. Little girl cries.*) Shut up, little girl! I didn't do anything!
MAN. You're crazy! (*This time the "You're crazy" remark rather than making her cry makes her livid with rage, and she grabs onto the Man's grocery cart. He grabs onto the other end—for protection—and she shakes the cart wildly, sort of growling in rage while she does so. She then runs off again, the Man staring after her.*)

BLACKOUT

Scene 3

Lights up again.

The Man looking at tuna.

The Woman comes into the supermarket again, making a beeline for where the Man is standing. Almost before she can get there, the little girl starts to cry offstage.

WOMAN. (*To crying offstage.*) Shut up, little girl, I didn't do anything yet! (*The Woman, irritated and stopped by the little girl's response, goes offstage again. The Man looks at the Woman very confused, not understanding why the little girl cried, or what the Woman was talking about. He looks out at the audience in befuddlement.*)

BLACKOUT

Scene 4

Lights up again.

The Man looking at tuna.

The Woman enters and makes a beeline to where the Man is standing. He senses her energy behind him, looks worried, and holds up a can of tuna to "study"—but then stops himself and decides on another tack.

MAN. (*Polite, reasonable.*) Is something the matter?
WOMAN. What?
MAN. Well, you seem . . . odd.
WOMAN. (*Enraged.*) Don't you talk to me that way, *asshole*! (*Hits him on the head; little girl starts crying.*) Shut up, little girl, I didn't do anything! (*Grabs the Man's grocery cart and says with glee:*) I'm crazy! (*The Woman chases the Man with his own grocery cart. He runs offstage in terror, she follows in shrieking pursuit.*)

BLACKOUT

Scene 5

Lights up again.

The Man looking at tuna.

The Woman enters once again, frustrated per usual.

The Man senses her presence.

The Woman overcomes her enormous frustration, and asks for what she wants.

WOMAN. Would you *please* move?
MAN. Are you trying to mug me? (*Turns and aims gun, shoots her dead; the little girl cries off-stage.*) Shut up, little girl! (*Aims gun off-stage, shoots little girl.*)

BLACKOUT

SCENE 6

The sound of waves. Lights up on a blank stage.

The Woman comes D. *in a spot and addresses the audience.*

WOMAN. There's so much violence in my dreams. I've been having this recurring dream about that stupid man in the tuna fish aisle. The other night I dreamed he shot me. (*The Man comes* D. *in another spot and addresses the audience. The Man and the Woman are seemingly not aware of one another.*)
MAN. I've been having this recurring dream about the woman in the supermarket. I dream that no matter how else I try to behave, she *always* hits me on the head. The other night, though, I dreamt I shot her. I liked that dream. Although not when I was dreaming it. It was upsetting then. (*The Man freezes during the Woman's next speech.*)
WOMAN. I dreamt I was back at Creedmoor, and one of the orderlies was saying to me, "The universe doesn't make sense, there is no order, you should be a star like Edie Sedgewick, but you're not." And then I was in the institution dining room, and all the other people at the table were being really disgusting with their food, so I didn't want to

look at this, so I kept staring at my plate. And on my plate there was this baked potato. And I started to get really afraid of this baked potato, and so finally I took my knife and fork to open it up and inside the baked potato was my father—who I didn't know very well, he left my mother and me when I was pretty young. And so I wanted to know how he was, but when I asked him he said, "Who are you, I don't know you." So I put butter on him and ate him. (*The Woman freezes during the Man's next speech.*)

MAN. The other night I dreamt my father was inside a baked potato. Isn't that strange? I was very startled to see him there, and I started to be afraid other people would see where my father was, and how small he was, so I kept trying to close the baked potato, but I guess the potato was hot, cause he'd start to cry when I'd shut the baked potato, so then I didn't know what to do. I thought of sending the whole plate back to the kitchen—tell the cook there's a person in my baked potato—but then I felt such guilt at deserting my father that I just sat there at the table and cried. He cried too. Then the waiter brought dessert, which was devil's food cake with mocha icing, and I ate that. Then I woke up, very hungry. I told my therapist about the dream, and he said that the baked potato represented either the womb or where I tried to put my father during the Oedipal conflict—"what Oedipal conflict?", I always say to him, "I won, hands down." And then my therapist said my father cried because he was unhappy, and that I dreamt about the cake because I was hungry. I think my therapist is an idiot. Maybe I should just have gurus. Or find a nutritionist. But what I'm doing now isn't working. (*Lights off the Man. The Woman is alone on-stage.*)

WOMAN. And then the night after my baked potato dream, I dreamt about that stupid man from the tuna fish aisle again, and in my dream I got so mad at him that I started to feel sorry for myself, but then Nazis started to chase me and I had to hide in the frozen foods counter. And then the next night I dreamt that I killed Sally Jessy Raphael.

MAN. (*From off-stage.*) And now the Sally Jessy Raphael Show. (*The stage transforms itself into a talk show setting. In the*

New York production, a section of the supermarket aisle turned around revealing a blue carpet and a blue "interview" chair; behind it was just more of the supermarket cans, but all color-coordinated blue—blue cans of soda, blue boxes of laundry detergent, etc., etc. Thus the setting rather than being a literal talk show became a kind of crackpot "dream" talk show, mixing up the supermarket and the TV show. The Woman discovers a microphone and red-framed glasses [similar to those worn by the real Sally Jessy Raphael], which she puts on.)
WOMAN. Hello. Sally Jessy Raphael can't be here today because I killed her. My aggression finally got the better of me, but what can you expect living in New York? These *are* her red-framed glasses, however. Do you like me in them? Now when my eyes are bloodshot from weeping or from allergies, you won't be able to tell whether it's my eyes that are red or my glasses!

This isn't my first time before the camera you know. The late Andy Warhol discovered me, and he said I should be as famous as Edie Sedgewick. That isn't very famous, of course, but those of you who follow the East Village scene and take drugs know who I mean. Ahahahahahahahaha haa.

I hope you don't mind if I do that, but I'm hoping to make that my signature on the air rather than these fuckin' glasses. Ahahahaha.

Let's see. Sally Jessy Raphael used to say "troops" a lot, I'll try that. Hey, troops! How are you? Do you like my glasses? That way when my eyes are red, you can't tell if I'm been crying or someone's punched me! Ahahahaha. Did I tell you about my father in the baked potato? I ate him. Now, troops, I don't mean sexually, I mean I ate him cannibalistically. Ahahahaha. Just kidding about that, troops, but know that my pain is sincere.

However, our show today isn't about cannibalism and it isn't about oral sex, although Dr. Ruth *is* a friend of mine . . . That's a lie, I hate Dr. Ruth and I hate Mother

Theresa! I want them to fight to the death with chains and nuclear-fueled revolving dildos! I'm sorry . . .

(*Calls out to technicians in the distance or off-stage.*) . . . can I say the word "dildo" on television? What? Read off the cards? Read off what cards? (*Sees something, reads from it.*) A E I O U. (*Tries to pronounce it.*) "Aeiou"? Well, that's an eye chart, not an idiot card. No, these cards are not useful. I am not an optimist. No, that's a slip of the tongue. I am not an optometrist. I am a talk show host or hostess.

Today our show is about nuclear proliferation. *And* it's also about the destruction of the ozone layer. *And* it's about sex education in the schools—should we tell our children about condoms or just wait until they get AIDS? And it's about AIDS, and it's about society's views on homosexuality—is it disgusting or is it delightful? And it's about the electoral college in our voting system—should we change it, should we rethink it, should we charge the delegates to the electoral college a tuition fee? And it's about free speech versus pay speech. Should people be allowed to say what they think? Should we demand that people who talk more pay more taxes? And it's about President Reagan and taxes. Does he know what he's talking about, or is he already dead?

Anyway, it's about all these topics—nuclear proliferation, condoms and children, the ozone layer, AIDS, homosexuality, heterosexuality, free speech, necrophilia and the presidency, and changing the electoral college—*and* we have to cover all these topics in under thirty minutes! So I better stop talking and bring out my first guest. Won't you join me in welcoming the Infant of Prague? (*Enter the Man dressed as the Infant of Prague. Now what do I mean by this? The Infant of Prague is a 17th-Century artist's invention of what the Christ Child, triumphant, might look like. Catholics are familiar with the look of this—usually in Infant of Prague statues—found in their churches, or sometimes on dashboards. Non-Catholics usually have not heard of the Infant of Prague, but some may recognize the "look." The "look" is this: a golden-haired child (of about ten to twelve maybe), dressed ornately. The most common look has white robes, embroidered with pearls and jewels, covered with a bright red cape, with white ruffles at the neck and wrists. On the top of the child's golden curls is a great big whopping crown, of gold and red, not unlike the crown in Imperial Margarine commercials on TV. [That is, it's big and has the "ball-like" red thing at the top of it.] The Infant in his left hand always carries a large orb [usually blue, and with a gold cross on top of it], and always has his right hand raised, with his first two fingers held upright, and his thumb and other two fingers folded in on one another. Since the Infant of Prague is usually a statue or sometimes a large doll whose silhouette often spreads out like an inverted "Y" due to the fullness of his robes, the New York designer chose to make the costume resemble a statue rather than a person. The robes spread out very wide to the side [on a kind of inner tubing] so that as costumed the Infant looked rather like an enormous, walking chess piece. When the audience saw underneath the Infant's robes, they saw a smooth, stretched white covering out of which two slippered feet protruded—again, looking very much like the bottom of a statue, and not that of a human being. Anyway, that, in words, is what the Infant of Prague looks like. And that is how the Man is dressed on his entrance. The Infant's personality, by the way, as played by the Man, is sunny and beatifically unflappable.)*

WOMAN. (*To herself.*) Why am I dreaming about the Infant of Prague? I don't even know what that is.

MAN. (*To audience; not in character as the Infant, and perhaps lowering his upraised right hand.*) I dreamt I was the Infant of Prague appearing on the Sally Jesse Raphael show, though I've never even heard of her. (*The Man raises his right hand, with its two upraised fingers, and resumes being the Infant.*)

WOMAN. Infant of Prague, won't you sit down?

MAN. Thank you, Sally, I only stand.

WOMAN. I'm not Sally. Sally is dead.

MAN. (*With sympathy.*) Oh. And is she in heaven with my father?

WOMAN. I really don't know. Enough chitchat. Tell me —"Infant of Prague"—is that your first name?

MAN. My name is the Infant of Prague, and I am a representation of the Christ Child.
WOMAN. Really. Where do you live?
MAN. I am housed in the Church of Our Lady of Victory in Prague, capital of Czechoslovakia.
WOMAN. (*A penetrating question.*) Where is Prague exactly?
MAN. It's in Czechoslovakia.
WOMAN. And where is Czechoslovakia?
MAN. (*Confused.*) It's in Prague.
WOMAN. Ahahahahahahaha! (*To Infant.*) That's my signature. Do you like my glasses? They're red. That way you can't tell if roving street gangs beat me up or not.
MAN. What?
WOMAN. Never mind. Tell us, Infant, a little bit about yourself. (*The Infant addresses a lot of his comments directly and happily to the audience because he is a born teacher, and because he is divine.*)
MAN. A statue of me was given to the Discalced Carmelites in Prague in 1628 by princess Polyxena Lobkowitz.
WOMAN. Polly who Lobka-what?
MAN. The statue was a gift from her mother, Maria Mariquez de Lara, who had brought the statue with her to Bohemia when she married the Czech nobleman, Vratsilav of Pernstyn.
WOMAN. Princeton? Princeton, New Jersey?
MAN. No, not Princeton. *Pern*-styn.
WOMAN. Uh huh. I wonder if I have any other guests that could come on. (*Calls off-stage.*) Oh, Ed? Is there anybody back there? (*To herself.*) Who's Ed? I don't know any Ed. Oh never mind. (*To Infant.*) Tell us, Infant, a little about what you're wearing. (*To audience.*) That's pretty wild, isn't it troops?
MAN. I'm glad you asked me that, Sally.
WOMAN. I'm not Sally. Sally's dead.
MAN. Then she's in heaven with my father. My inner garments are similar to the priest's alb, and are made of white linen and of lace. (*Proudly shows a bit of his undergarments, or beneath a ruffle.*)

WOMAN. Ooooh, this is getting racy.
MAN. Please don't make sacrilegeous remarks or I'll have to leave.
WOMAN. I always get the difficult guests. First Eartha Kitt, and now a tea cozy.
MAN. (*Turning as in a fashion show.*) Covering my inner garments is a miniature liturgical cope, made of heavy damask, richly woven with gold and embroidered with pearls. (*In the New York production, the Woman actually went out into the audience to ask her questions, rather as Phil Donahue and Sally Jessy Raphael often do.*)
WOMAN. Wow, you could really feed a lot of starving people with that outfit there, couldn't you, Infant?
MAN. (*Firmly.*) Most people do not eat gold and pearls, Sally.
WOMAN. Sally's dead, how many times do I have to tell you that!
MAN. Three times, representing the Blessed Trinity. Father, Son and Holy Spirit.
WOMAN. (*Referring to the orb.*) What's that little paperweight in your hand?
MAN. This is not a paperweight. It is a miniature globe, signifying the world-wide kingship of the Christ Child.
WOMAN. Uh huh. Well, fine, let's move on, shall we? (*A glint in her eye.*) Let's talk about condoms for a bit. Your church isn't very big on condoms, is it?
MAN. When people ask me, the Infant of Prague, for advice on sexuality, I sometimes think to myself, what do I know about sex?—I'm an infant. What's more, I'm the Infant of Prague; I can't sit down, let alone have sex. (*Laughs goodnaturedly at his quip.*) But what people don't realize sometimes is that God my father has a holy and blessed purpose to the mystery of sexuality, and that purpose is to create other little infants like myself to glorify God and creation. That is why condoms are wrong because anything that intercepts—or *contra*-cepts—this process is deeply wrong.
WOMAN. Now let's get real here for a second, Infant. People are always going to have sex, and now we have this deadly disease AIDS which is killing people, and one of the

ways to protect oneself is to use a condom. Now don't you think we better get *practical* here, and get people to use condoms? Whaddya say, Infant of Prague???
MAN. We must instruct the people at risk to abstain from sex.
WOMAN. Oh, well, fine. And we can tell the waterfall to stop falling, but is that practical?
MAN. Moses parted the Red Sea. (*Smiles at the audience, having made an unassailable point.*)
WOMAN. Uh huh. So let's get this straight—you would prefer that adolescents die from AIDS rather than tell them about condoms?
MAN. I do not prefer this at all, Sally. Yes, I know, Sally is dead. Sorry, I keep forgetting. Sally, I would tell all the teenagers of the world to be like me, an infant without sexual urges, until they were much, much older and ready to commit to one person for life, and to glory in the sacramental beauty of sex, within marriage, where during the actual act of intercourse all you can think about is "Procreation! Procreation! I am going to have a little baby, a little infant to glorify God!"
WOMAN. Well the teenagers in New Jersey are gonna love that answer. *Come on, Infant.* Don't you think you're a *little* impractical.
MAN. The Divine *is* impractical, that's why it's divine. (*The Infant smiles delightedly, another unassailable point. The Woman would like to kill him.*)
WOMAN. (*To audience.*) We have to take a little break here but we'll be right back with more of the Infant of Prague. (*ON THE AIR sign goes off; and theme music starts. Off the air, the Woman unleashes her pent-up fury and begins to pummel the Infant.*) YOU JERK, YOU STUBBORN SHIT, YOU EFFEMINATE EUNUCH, YOU MAKE ME WANT TO VOMIT WITH YOUR HOLIER THAN THOU ATTITUDE! WHY SHOULD WE LISTEN TO YOU ABOUT SEX??? YOU'RE AFRAID OF SEX, YOUR IDEAS ON SEX ARE RIGID AND INSANE, AND SOMEONE SHOULD HAVE YOU KILLED! I WANT YOU *DEAD!* DIE, DIE, DIE! (*The Infant looks startled and alarmed during this outburst. Towards the end of her outburst, one of her hits*

makes him fall over backwards, and the Woman dives on top of him, continuing her pummelling. The ON-THE-AIR sign comes back on, as does the theme music. The Woman looks out, caught in the act of straddling and beating up her guest. She gets off of him, and talks to the camera. The Infant remains on the ground, unable to stand up due to the weight of his clothes and crown. He struggles from time to time, moving his slippered feet about pathetically.) Well, we're back on the air now. Ahahahahaha. Let's *talk* about "air," and the ozone layer, shall we? (*Notices the Infant's struggling; explains to the camera.*) He fell down during the commercial.
MAN. Would you help me stand up please?
WOMAN. Wait a minute. Give me your opinion on the destruction of the ozone layer.
MAN. I am opposed to the destruction of the ozone layer, Sally.
WOMAN. Who did we tell you was dead?
MAN. Sally.
WOMAN. Right answer. Alright, I'll help you up now. (*The Woman helps the Infant stand up. He looks disoriented for a moment.*) Okay. Let's go for the "gold." What about homosexuality—is it disgusting or is it delightful?
MAN. It is a grievous sin. But I love homosexuals, I just want them to be celibate until they die.
WOMAN. Who booked this jerk on here anyway??? (*Calls off-stage again.*) Ed, I'm talking to you!
MAN. Where is Sally?
WOMAN. Who is Ed?
MAN. I don't want to be interviewed by you anymore. (*Starts to wander toward off-stage and to call out.*) Sally? Sally!
WOMAN. (*Takes out a gun and aims it at him.*) I killed Sally Jessy Raphael, and I can kill you! (*Shoots him several times.*)
MAN. It is not possible to kill the Infant of Prague. (*He exits happily. She is enraged.*)
WOMAN. (*Calling off after him.*) I hate you, I hate you, you Infant of Prague! (*To audience.*) I hate religious bigots. And I hate people who think they know what's right. And I hate people who are filled with hate. And I hate people who are filled with love. I wish my mother had had me killed when I

was a fetus. That's the kind of person I am. Do you get it? Ahahahahahaha!

WOMAN's VOICE. (*On tape.*) My next guest today is Rama Sham Rama.

WOMAN. I don't want no fucking next guest! (*Shoots her gun off-stage, apparently stopping Rama Sham Rama; then calls off in the other direction.*) Ed!! You're fired! (*Shoots her gun off in Ed's direction. The theme music plays nightmarishly, and the talk show set disappears or recedes into the distance. The Woman is now back in her waking-dream state again, and addresses the audience as herself once more, out of her Sally dream.*) Why is there so much violence in my dreams? I'm always killing people or they're killing me. The other night I dreamt I killed Sally Jessy Raphael. And then I tried to kill the Infant of Prague, whoever the hell that is. Then Rama Sha Rambus somebody. I have to let go of this rage, I can't live this way anymore. (*Lights off the Woman, spot on the Man, dressed back in his normal clothes again.*)

MAN. I dreamt the other night that I was in Central Park before dawn at the Harmonic Convergence ceremony, and that the "icky woman" was talking about her hopes for mankind again, but that various mental patients kept interrupting her. (*Lights back on the Woman. The Man's spot stays on also, though he doesn't yet hear what she's saying.*)

WOMAN. I dreamt that I was at the "Harmonic Convergence"—whatever the hell that is. Something is wrong with my dreams lately, I keep dreaming about things I've never heard about. Anyway, and this woman with a flower in her head kept saying things like "I dance for the Sun King," and "I dance for the Moon King"—it made me *real* hostile. So I called out at the top of my lungs, "Why don't you get your tooth fixed?"

MAN. Oh! And then I dreamt that the woman from the tuna fish aisle was there, and she shouted at the "icky woman," "Why don't you see a dentist?" or "there's something wrong with your tooth," or something like that. But it didn't make much sense, there wasn't anything wrong with the woman's tooth.

WOMAN. And then all these aging hippies were sitting

with their legs crossed and their eyes closed, doing meditation . . . (*The Man closes his eyes and puts his arms at his sides, palms out, joining in the meditation.*) . . . and I yelled out, "WHAT DO YOU THINK THIS IS—1967???" And then someone gave me a flower, and I said "Oh, fuck you!" and I ripped the flower up, and they had this real hurt look on their face, and then everyone started to make sounds together . . .

MAN. (*Toning, a low, calm sound.*) Ohhhhhhhhhhhhhh-mmmmmmmmmmmmmmmmm . . . (*Continues toning.*)

WOMAN. Ohhhhhhhhhhhmmmmmmmmmmmmmmm. So then I did that for a while. But I got bored, so I thought, I know, I'll pretend to be a car alarm, so I went: eeeeeeeeeeeeeeeEEEEEEEEEEEEEEEEEEEEEEEEEEEE-EEEEEEEEEEEEEEEEEEEEEEE . . .

(*Woman does an upsettingly successful imitation of a shrieking car alarm. The Man seems to hear it in his unconscious, and it fights with his "ohm" sound. He frowns.*)

MAN. (*Continuing through above.*) . . . mmmmmmmm-mmmmmmmmmmmm. Then I turned *off* my alarm . . . (*Makes a gesture of turning off alarm; the Woman stops making her noise.*) . . . which was waking me, but then I went right back to sleep, and now the "icky woman" wasn't there anymore, and somehow I had been designated the person who was supposed to run the ceremony in her absence. I tried to blow on a conch shell, which I thought I had in my hand, but it was actually a ham sandwich, so, of course, when I blew on it it didn't make any noise. So then I addressed the crowd. (*Lights shift. The Man crosses* C. *The sound of a light wind, and of tinkling wind chimes. The Woman is seated nearby. He and she are now in a kind of joint dream about the Harmonic Convergence. In the New York production, a black backdrop moved away, and the setting was a dream-like setting of Central Park, with bushes and shrubbery around, mixed in strangely with parts of the supermarket aisle and some of the elements of the talk show as well. It was lit like night, a bit before dawn. The man speaks to crowd, a bit loudly projected.*) I seem to have misplaced my conch shell. If anyone finds it, please let me know.

WOMAN. (*Disruptively loud.*) WHAT THE FUCK'S A CONCH SHELL?
MAN. (*Trying to pay no attention.*) I have been asked to lead the ceremony until dawn comes. The icky woman—that is . . . Vicki, her name is Vicki—has had to leave the park to take several patients back to various mental institutions.
WOMAN. Was any of them Creedmoor? I have connections at Creedmoor.
MAN. (*To Woman, patiently, but bothered.*) Please, don't just call out, I find it disorienting.
WOMAN. Why don't you get your tooth fixed?
MAN. There is nothing wrong with my tooth. (*To crowd.*) We are here to enter a new age. The planets of Mars and . . . hathor are in alignment with the seventh moon of the seventh sun of the seventh seal.
WOMAN. Why don't you give me a job?
MAN. Please everyone hold a crystal to your head, and align yourself with mother earth. (*Holds a small clear crystal to his head, and closes his eyes to concentrate.*)
WOMAN. If you hire me at the magazine, I promise not to write "pig" on the wall with your blood!
MAN. I would not be willing to hire you under those circumstances.
WOMAN. Well, fuck you!
MAN. Can someone take this woman away? Is Vicki back?
WOMAN. Vicki's dead. She and Mother Theresa fought to the death with knives at the colliseum.
MAN. (*Closes his eyes, does his "affirmation" hands-in-a-circular-motion gestures.*) Everyone in my universe is cooperative. I am a natural leader, and no one yells out in the middle of my speaking. I let the gems of the earth empower me. (*Holds the crystal to his forehead.*)
WOMAN. Why are you holding that piece of chandelier to your forehead?
MAN. It's a crystal.
WOMAN. And my doctors think *I'm* crazy.
MAN. Would you please be quiet?

WOMAN. No! (*Sings "Vilia"* operatically, to annoy the man, and to block out what he's saying.*)
MAN. (*Trying to ignore her.*) The earth is entering a *new phase* where it is going to evaluate what man has done to it over the past many centuries. And, if there are 144,000 *enlightened people* on the earth at the time of the Harmonic Convergence, it's possible we can shift away from death and destruction . . .
WOMAN. I dance for the sun king! (*Dances across the stage in a put-on, arty way.*)
MAN. . . . to a place of unity, and unconditional love and harmony . . .
WOMAN. I dance for the moon king! (*Dances some more.*)
MAN. . . . both for mankind and for the planet.
WOMAN. And when I don't dance, I laugh. Ahahahahahahahaha!
MAN. We only have a few minutes left until dawn.
WOMAN. (*Suddenly direct; to the Man.*) You're blocking my way.
MAN. We should all be silent now, until the dawn.
WOMAN. You're blocking my way.
MAN. What?
WOMAN. Why are you always blocking my way to the tuna fish?
MAN. What tuna fish? There isn't any tuna fish here. We're in Central Park.
WOMAN. Well, what's that then? (*She points* U. *where, indeed, there is a section of supermarket aisle with tuna fish cans on it, mixed in with the Central Park shrubbery. The Man is very disoriented. There had been no tuna fish in his Central Park dream up till now.*)
MAN. *Very annoyed, to the crowd.*) Why is there tuna fish in Central Park??
WOMAN. It's a Gristedes. It's very convenient.
MAN. No, we all have to cooperate now, this isn't the time for tuna fish.
WOMAN. I want to get by you!

---

*See Special Note on copyright page.

MAN. No, we have to prepare for the dawn.
WOMAN. I make the dawn come up like thunder!
MAN. No! Now go sit down and wait. Can't you do that?
WOMAN. I'm always being told to wait. When is it my turn??
MAN. NEVER! NOW SIT THE FUCK DOWN!!! (*The Woman is startled by the Man's fury. She sits. He goes into toning, somewhat abruptly after his screaming.*) Ohhhhhhh-hhhhhhhmmmmmmmmmmmmmmmmm. . . .
WOMAN. (*Hands over ears, hating the sound.*) Stop making that noise! (*The Man continues to tone. The Woman is driven crazy by the sound. She stands and makes her "car alarm" sound again. She crosses to him, dream-like, raises her fist in slow motion and brings it down on his head. He falls to the ground, and she is now free to get to the tuna fish finally. All sound stops. The Woman runs over to the tuna fish aisle, thrilled.*) At last! I'm here now, I'm safe, I'm here, I have what I want! (*Takes a can, reads it.*) Poison. (*Throws it offstage; looks at next one.*) Poison. (*Throws it offstage; looks at next one.*) Poison! (*Throws it; looks at next one.*) *Salmon. I don't want salmon. (Throws it; looks at next one.*) Poison! (*Throws it; looks at next one.*) Tomato soup! (*Throws it.*) WHAT IS THE MATTER WITH THIS STORE??? (*Weeps. The Woman moves away from the aisle. The stage darkens. In New York, a black backdrop came in and swallowed up the whole Central Park-supermarket setting. The Man starts to come to from having been hit. He rubs his head, and notices the darkening around him.*)
MAN. Oh, everything's turning black. Keep toning. Ohhhhhhhhhhhhhhhhhhhhhmmmmmmmmm. . . . (*The Woman's weeping continues. The sound of the little girl crying off-stage is heard also, nightmarishly. The Man keeps trying to tone, to drown out the sound of crying.*) If people are going to refuse to tone, the dawn may not come up. Ohhhhhhhhhhhhhhhhmmmmmm. Ohhhhhhhhhhhmmm-mm. (*To weeping Woman.*) SHUT UP! (*The lights shift to two spotlights, one on the Man, one on the Woman. All noise stops.*)
WOMAN. (*To audience.*) And then I dreamt that the man in the tuna fish aisle was suddenly empathetic with me.
MAN. (*To audience.*) And then I dreamt that the woman and I were still in Central Park and she was still weeping,

but I felt this sudden wave of empathy for her. (*The lights shift back to how they were before the asides. The Woman goes back to weeping, but the scene is otherwise quiet. The Man tries to think how to speak to her.*) What's the matter?
WOMAN. I'm laughing wild amid severest woe.
MAN. But you're weeping.
WOMAN. Oh, sorry. (*Burst of crazy laughter.*) Ahahahahahahahahahaha!
MAN. Did you get the tuna fish you need?
WOMAN. Why don't you get your tooth fixed?
MAN. Ummmm . . . That's a good suggestion, thank you, I will.
WOMAN. The tuna fish is all mislabeled. Some of it is salmon, and some of it is poison, and some of it is tomato soup.
MAN. That's a shame. Maybe you would like to tell the people here in the park about your hopes for the Harmonic Convergence?
WOMAN. Yes, I would. (*Addresses the crowd; with a soft quality.*) I hope that the pounding in my head stops. And I hope that people will not spit on me as I pass them in the street. And I hope that someone gives me a job. And I hope that I have more good days than bad days. That I learn to say this glass is half full, it is not half empty. And to hell with my half full glass—I want a *full* full glass, I want it overflowing. And I want to feel joy like I did that one summer day for ten minutes right before I decided life was horrible and I went crazy. I want to recapture the feeling of *liking* to be alive. I want to feel joy that looks like this. (*She throws her head back and spreads her arms wide in an exuberant, open, receiving position. The darkness on the stage changes to vibrant color: deep purple to deep red to a warm, rose hue. In other words, it's dawn, though not presented realistically. The Man notices the light. He stands and feels he should probably continue "leading" the crowd.*)
MAN. Everybody breathe. In . . . (*The Woman is in her exuberant, head-thrown-back posture still. Without making it a big deal, she automatically joins the Man's, and crowd's, breathing rhythms.*)
WOMAN. And out. . . . (*The Man notes her joining. Again,*

no big deal, but it's the first time they've had agreement on anything ever. There is relief. Breathing, dawn.)
MAN. In . . .
WOMAN. . . . and out . . . (*The Man and the Woman maybe look at one another on their last lines, before the lights fade.*)
MAN. In . . .
WOMAN. . . . and out . . .

PROPERTY LIST

1. LAUGHING WILD

Chair
Bag
Purse

2. SEEKING WILD

Chair
Small table
Pitcher of water
Half full glass of water
Very large hand-painted canvas poster of an Egyptian Eye
Sphere
Pyramid
Lectern/stand
Crystals
3x5 cards
Polaroid pictures

3. DREAMING WILD

Tuna fish cans
Shopping cart
Handgun (Man)
2 blue chairs
Table
Ashtray
Boom microphone
Red framed glasses
Hand held microphone
Infant of Prague orb
Handgun (Woman)
Cans of poison
Can of salmon
Can of tomato soup
Foliage
Black crystal
2 pieces of paper (with writing on them)
Clear crystal

Eggs, butter, cheese. Return phone calls to Jon Denny, Jay Siem at Merrill Lynch, Nancy Quinn at the Young Playwrights Festival. Answer letter from three years ago asking me to speak on Whither American Drama at the University of Rochester. Buy triple A batteries for my VCR remote control.

I went to a restaurant the other day and read David Mamet's "Writing in Restaurants." I ordered Eggs Benedict, and spilled Hollandaise Sauce on the book. It was a sign of something, but of what?

Last year I was re-experiencing my feelings of grief and deep sorrow at feeling (or being) abandoned at age 3, when my mother went into a deep depression at the death of her second child and my father was stopping up his feelings by drinking. This year I am about to re-live parts of my adolescence. Along these lines, I have grown my first beard; it has bits of gray in it, which is not appropriate for a teenager, but is fine for a man of my age.

Some days I want to kill Frank Rich, the drama critic of the New York times. He represents this Great Deaf Ear I must somehow get through to in order to reach a theatregoing public. The "New Age" part of me knows this perception regarding him is merely a giving away of my power to him; and, truthfully, in New York I seem to have an audience that comes to my plays regardless, more or less, of what he says.

The genuine problem I face is that the approval and hoopla of the Times is very important to creating an "atmosphere" around a play, a sense that one should see it soon; and this "must see" quality is what sells tickets at the beginning, and motivates a producer to move a play from a non-profit New York theatre (like Playwrights Horizons or Manhattan Theatre Club) to a commercial run on or off-Broadway. After a couple of months, this Times' support is much less important, and then word of mouth kicks in. But for that initial period, the Times support is awfully significant. And having your play in an open commercial run, verses a few weeks at a non-profit theatre, is of enormous difference in terms of reaching a larger audience, and of finances. (You can make a living with royalties from a play that runs; you can pay maybe two months rent with payment from a play at a non-profit theatre.)

Oh Lord, I really don't want to talk about the critics particularly, because I don't see a solution in sight; and yet every time I sit down to work on the notes for this play the issue comes charging up for me.

Everyone in theatre knows how crazy it is to have One Critical Voice that carries such weight, and that it's the result of having only one newspaper that most of the theatre-going public seems to read; and it's pointless to blame anyone because nobody "caused" this state of affairs. But most people in theatre suffer severely under this state of affairs.

Nothing similar exists in movies or books because they are reviewed nationally, and quickly a consensus forms. For instance, Woody Allen's film "Hannah and Her Sisters" received a very ho-hum response from Pauline Kael in the New Yorker. The bulk of the other reviews indicated a consensus that "Hannah" was one of his best films, and Kael's opinion quickly fit into its proper place as an idiosyncratic nay vote. If "Hannah" had been a play and the gifted Ms. Kael had been the New York Times theatre critic, "Hannah" would probably have closed.

The truth is I'm worn out working in this system. Of my last four plays—"Beyond Therapy," "Baby with the Bathwater," "The Marriage of Bette and Boo," and "Laughing Wild"—the Times (in the Pontiff-like voice of Rich) only liked "Baby with the Bathwater," and that, due to his review, was the one that came closest to being moved to a commercial run. However, it was the one that least should have been considered for a commercial run since audiences *way* preferred the other three, especially "Beyond Therapy," which most people found very funny, and "Bette and Boo," which most found funny and touching.

I've twice now had ecstatic receptions to plays on opening nights—"Bette and Boo" and "Laughing Wild"—that are impossible for me to enjoy because I know I'm waiting for the word from his Lord Chief Executioner. It's such a stupid system. If he didn't write for the major newspaper in New York, Frank Rich's opinion per se would be of zero interest to me, especially as the years have gone on and he's gotten harder and harder and harder. It must be all that veal he eats at Orso's.

Now one can buck the system to a point. If a producer is aggressive and pours money into a campaign and gets the actors to take lower salaries and gets the writer, director and designers to waive their royalties (and everyone is getting low salaries to begin with), you can keep a show open until it finds its audience. Jack McQuiggan, producer of Larry Shue's "The Foreigner," did that in recent years. So did the producers of Shue's "The Nerd." More power to these people.

In my situation I've mostly been working with the New York non-profit theatres which have subscription seasons of plays so that a play must either be so acclaimed that it moves to a different theatre (a commercial house on or off Broadway), or it must close to make room for the next play. So in those houses—Playwrights Horizons, Manhattan Theatre Club, the Public Theatre (though Joe Papp has a bit more flexibility, having more spaces)—one cannot keep a play running open-ended until an audience "finds" it. One must be acclaimed, with the accompanying hoopla causing a flurry of box office activity that pretty much demands a move to a commercial run—which is indeed what happened with my play "Sister Mary Ignatius Explains It All For You" at Playwrights Horizons in 1981. Without the critical Times hoopla, you most likely will close in a few weeks to make room for the next play.

Now in a "this glass is half full, not half empty" scenario, I must admit I get my plays produced, and I make a living. So what more do I want?

Well, the truth is, I do want more. I want to work in a theatrical arena where one man's opinion does not carry this crazy weight, where if audiences and other critics find "Beyond Therapy" funny, Mr. Rich's opinion that it is not funny will not count except as a tiny part of a larger consensus. But seemingly I can't have that. The Times is totally unmoving about "taking responsibility" for its power. People from the theatre community have been meeting with its editors on and off for at least 20 years; and the Times prides itself on being open to solving this problem, and claims to be embarrassed by its power. But the possible solutions to the problem—having more than one critic review a play at a time, running a "scorecard" of what the other critics said, even a tiny suggestion like having "opinion" written at the top of the review—are invariably overruled by the Times. The truth is, whether they admit it to themselves or not, the editors of the Times and Rich love their power. It makes them feel, well, powerful.

So, in truth, to overcome Frank Rich I have to either work with more aggressive producers (like the afore-mentioned McQuiggan, who bucked the critical rejection of "The Foreigner" to keep it running until audiences found it, thereby making his property very valuable, and produced all over the country), or somehow be satisfied with a 4 week run at a non-profit theatre in New York.

But right now I feel worn out by the notion. I don't want to go up in front of His Pontiff Rich again. Theatre seems an unfriendly and unaccepting arena to work in, at least in New York. I can't seem to see around this problem right now. I've recently had good times writing for camera—a half hour episode of PBS' Trying Times series called "The Visit" and starring Swoosie Kurtz, and a crackpot 7 minute film for Showtime's "By-line" series that was a mock documentary of my life as a writer (with Christine Estabrook as my wife who sleeps on the kitchen floor). It was fun to make these works, and to know there was no one-man pit bull waiting to devour them. Maybe it's time to hand the theatre over to Rich—let him order it just like his veal and pasta at Orso's.

I love theatre, which is why there's anger (and sorrow) in

my tone for what I perceive Rich and the Times to have done to New York theatre, and to my possible place in it. It's just not a good place here.

Christopher Durang
New York City
March 1988

REGARDING UPDATES
January, 1996

I wrote *Laughing Wild* in 1987, and I allowed myself to make a lot of then current references.

I did the play again in Los Angeles in 1990, and at that time cut or changed references that seemed too dated (especially regarding President Reagan).

The emotions behind the play — the difficulty of living amidst our urban cities' intensities; looking for meaning in life — do not seem likely to date anytime soon. Some of the specific references, though, do continue to date.

So the following is my list of changes I made from Los Angeles in 1990, and a few new changes I'm making now.

At the end of the changes, I've enclosed some thoughts on what things might need to change in the future; and I've explained some of the changes I've already made; and I offer a couple of thoughts about acting interpretations of the play.

The page numbers refer to the Dramatists Play Service acting script.

LAUGHING WILD

The Woman's Monologue

1. Pg. 7: "they cost about $2.50 in the movie theatre".

Either leave as is, or change to "$3.50", as you see fit.

2. Pg. 11: — the first reference to Sally Jessy Raphael.

Change the paragraph that starts with "And speaking of which, who is Sally Jessy Raphael?" to the following:

> "And speaking of which, who is Sally Jessy Raphael, and more importantly, why is she? Does anyone know? I have a television in my apartment, I don't have a bed, but I have trouble sleeping anyway, sometimes I sleep in the bathtub; but originally she was on at three in the morning, or something; now she's on at 10 or 4 or 3, her time is always changing, that is, Sally Jessy Raphael's is; and I guess she's supposed to be a kind of female Phil Donahue. But my point is, who is she? Why does she think she's interesting, or that we should listen to her?" (etc., as written)

3. Pg. 14: — reference to Pearl Bailey.

Change to:

> "I've seen Pearl Bailey and Diana Ross do that, it's really obnoxious. I want to see them killed. Well actually Pearl Bailey is dead. I'd like to be dead.

"Tell me, are you enjoying my company ..." (etc. as written)

4. Pg. 14: — first reference to Dr. Ruth Westheimer.

Change to:

"I have the most wonderful doctors, they're all like Dr. Ruth Westheimer on television. Dr. Ruth Westheimer. And they wonder why I have reality testing problems. Don't you find her peculiar? Andy Warhol said everyone would be famous for fifteen minutes in the twentieth century ..." (etc. as written)

5. Pg. 15: "Ronald Reagan hung upside down," "Mayor Koch made to eat Westway."

Cut the Mayor Koch beat entirely. Change the Reagan reference to the following:

"... just like Siskel and Ebert dismissing a particularly dreadful movie; and then I want Jesse Helms hung upside down over sulfur emissions and made to inhale toxic waste, just like those animals who are made to smoke three million cigarettes; and then I want the world to come to a complete and total end, ka-plooey, ka-ploppy, ka-plopp! AHHAHAHAHAHAHAHAHAHAHAHAHAHAHAHA!"

THINKING WILD

The Man's Monologue

6. Pg. 24: — References to Secretary of Education, Environment, etc., under Reagan.

Cut all these references. Change to the following:

> "And there's acid rain and something wrong with the ozone layer, and global warming, and destruction of the rain forests. God, it's discouraging.
>
> "And think about God...." (etc. as written)

7. Pg. 25: — Barbara Bach, Lorenzo Lamas, etc.

Let's update these as follows:

> "Sometimes I have nightmares about the upper bodies of Sharon Stone and Marky Mark. People whose first and last names begin with the same letter. Marky Mark. Suzanne Somers. Lorenzo Lamas. Madonna."

Note: if you prefer the "Cher" joke in the original script rather than "Madonna," that's fine with me. Or "Fabia" would work as a one-name joke. And if you prefer the old names, that's fine, too. The only one that feels way too dated right now seems to me to be Barbara Bach.

8. Pg. 26: — reference to NASA.

Cut the reference, or leave it — up to you.

The Man was referring to the spaceship that blew up with teachers in it. That's no longer so recent, so I leave it up to you whether it's effective for the Man — in his somewhat speedy free association at this point — to bring it up. But the sentence would make sense with the NASA phrase dropped.

9. Pg. 27: "recent Supreme Court ruling."

Drop the word "recent." Change to:

> "And things like the Supreme Court ruling that sex between consenting adult homosexuals ..." (etc. as written)

[Note: for your information, this refers to the Supreme Court case *Hardwicke v. Bower* in 1985, decided 5–4; the majority side held that it was OK for a state to choose to criminalize sexual behavior between *consenting adults in private* if the state felt like it. And it quoted Biblical injunctions against homosexuality as one of the legal justifications. The specific case had to do with two men, in the privacy of their bedroom, who were intruded upon, by mistake, by some person who then had them arrested on the basis of anti-sodomy laws on the books. In their bedroom with their doors closed. A shockingly intrusive decision in my opinion.]

10. Pg. 27: "Meese Commission", "milk at a 7-Eleven store."

The Meese Commission reference is too tied to the Reagan years. The reference to 7-Eleven may have been forgotten: the government got behind raiding 7-Eleven Stores if they carried *Playboy,* thus making them stop carrying that magazine.

So instead change that section to the following:

> "At intermission the ushers will let you look at them! ... although I suppose some pornography commission

will rush in here and try to take them away from you and then force you to watch reruns of *Lassie* on the Family Channel. God, I took some Valium before I came out here, but it hasn't calmed me down a bit." (etc. as written)

11. Pg. 32-33: — the Harmonic Convergence.

This event, which occurred in 1987, has certainly left public memory. However, I think it's fine that the Man remembers it. But I have changed some of the tenses, and dropped the reference to 1987; it's better now to leave it vague when it happened.

Also, for length, I have dropped most of the paragraph beginning "We went over to 6th Avenue," moving on to "... predictably we got an absolutely terrifying taxi driver" faster.

So here is an updated version of the first half of the Harmonic Convergence stuff:

> (pg. 32:) " ... Albert Camus was not a laugh riot. You know, years ago I went to the Harmonic Convergence ceremony in Central Park. You probably don't remember what that even was anymore. Well, it was this strange, New Age-connected belief, prophesied in several ancient cultures — the Mayan, the Aztec, Hopi Indians — that said that August 16th and 17th of this one specific year represented a window in time in which the planets all lined up in some special way or other, and that, supposedly, there was an opportunity for mankind to make a spiritual shift away from pollution and destruction of the planet back to being "in alignment" with mother earth, and so on.
>
> "The newspapers made fun of the event at the time, (etc. this paragraph as written)

> "So a couple of friends and I — I'm starting to have more friends who think this way —" (etc. as written)... "Or at least as a place where people were going to gather."
>
> "We went to hail a cab, and predictably we got an absolutely terrifying taxi driver. He'd race up to every red light...." (etc. as written)

Note: so basically I've put the early stuff in the past tense, taken out the specific year, and cut the paragraph about "we went over to 6th Avenue".

12. Pg. 35: — reference to "Columbus Ave". The Man looks at the Eye poster and says: "It looks Egyptian. Or Columbus Ave. I shouldn't make fun of it."

Explanation: In New York, "Columbus Avenue" was a yuppie-ish part of the city with trendy, arty shops in it. That, though, is too local a reference (and it's less true now too, I think).

So in L.A. I changed Columbus Avenue to "Sante Fe," referring to a type of design. (The poster happened to have a lot of turquoise blue and gold.) That worked there, and may work other places. Or right now I also thought of "It looks Egyptian. Or like Shakti Gawain's wall paper." (She's a New Age writer.) Would that work for you?

DREAMING WILD

The Third Part

13. Pg. 43: — reference to President Reagan and taxes. Cut the reference and change to the following:

> "... Should people be allowed to say what they think? Should we demand that people who talk more pay more taxes? And where would that leave me?
>
> "Anyway, it's about all these topics — nuclear proliferation, condoms and children, the ozone layer, AIDS, homosexuality, heterosexuality, free speech, a tax on people who talk too much, and changing the electoral college — *and* we have to cover all these topics in under thirty minutes!..." (etc. as written)

Those are the specific updates I offer as of January 1996. I offer some thoughts on the need for future ones, and some explanations, and some acting thoughts, on the following pages.

FUTURE CHANGES IN "LAUGHING WILD"

Mother Theresa, Sally Jessy Raphael, Dr. Ruth Westheimer.

The Woman's dislike of these three people is to me important to her character.

I think all 3 public figures still function strongly in the play as the focus for her sometimes sensible, sometimes irrational feelings. And I feel they have not dated, or fallen from public consciousness.

At some later point, if Mother Theresa is known to be seriously ill or when she dies, then I think references to her would have to change.

Presently, one could just replace her mentions with a mention of "The Pope" (though that would be less effective). But that possible change will only hold as long as "The Pope" remains extremely conservative theologically, as the present Pope John Paul II is. If a future Pope should be more liberal (especially on sexual matters), then this switch of reference would no longer work.

If at a future time, neither the Mother Theresa reference nor the Pope reference works, please feel free to contact me directly care of my agent or care of the Dramatists Play Service.

But for now, keep as written.

The references to Sally Jessy and Dr. Ruth seem likely to last longer — though if something changes about the public's perception of them, it's possible they would need to be changed as well.

There was a period during which Sally Jessy Raphael had two very public tragedies regarding her son and daughter. During that period, I think it would have been hard to do this play, because the references to Sally Jessy would have made the audience think of the sadness in her life.

To my surprise, I think Sally Jessy's public persona as a chatty, somewhat self-consciously sympathetic talk show host has reasserted itself in the public's mind; so I think she still works in the play as of 1996.

I can imagine a time in the future when she might not, however. So, once again, I invite you to contact me if an updating seems necessary.

Finally, regarding Dr. Ruth. The Woman (and I) seem to be correct that Dr. Ruth is lasting way beyond her Warhol-allotted 15 minutes. Indeed, I learned from a Swiss production of this play that Dr. Ruth is indeed known in both Germany and Switzerland as well. And I learned she has her own CD-Rom.

Once again, though, if something major happens that changes our public perception of Dr. Ruth, one might have to come up with a substitution for her too. Since we don't have another cheery-folksy sex educator presently on our horizon, God knows what replacement would be available. But who knows in the future? So again, feel free to approach me at a future date if Dr. Ruth no longer seems apt.

(In the previous changes I have adjusted the first paragraph on Dr. Ruth ... she once had a TV show entitled *Good Sex,* but it is no longer on; and the title has faded from everyone's memory, including mine. So that reference is cut.)

A FEW STRAY UPDATING ISSUES

THE REFERENCE TO *PASSWORD*

I'd like to leave this reference as it is. It is true that for the past several years, *Password* has not been on the air. But it really is the rules of that game that are funniest for the Woman's fantasy of what Dr. Ruth would say.

Plus, we can assume that the Woman is old enough that she would remember *Password.*

For those audience members who don't know the specific game, I would prefer that they intuit what the game was like, rather than use a more current TV game whose rules are not the same.

In 5 to 10 years, I might possibly feel differently. Though at that point, maybe the whole play should be done as a period piece, and updating in general won't seem appropriate. One could then set it in 1987, and even go back to the Reagan references. But for now, I think updating it a bit is the best idea; but I prefer to leave *Password* alone.

JESSE HELMS

At this point, I suggested changing the line about Reagan being hung upside down over sulfur emissions to the same image but with Jesse Helms instead, since he is known as a supporter of tobacco interests in his state of North Carolina, and known to be very right-wing on issues of the environment.

I also thought of saying "Dan and Marilyn Quayle" at this point; or "Pat Buchanan". I also thought of Newt Gingrich, but strangely he's become so dominant and evocative of 1995-96 that I found him too current — I need the play to be generally in the present, but not feel like its references are literally yesterday. (Because one such reference may make the audience unconsciously wonder why the Woman doesn't make more immediate references.)

But basically the person chosen should either be a known enemy of environmental protection; or a person (like the Quayles) who is known as extremely right-wing conservative, who most likely tends to favor business over environment.

And I apologize for the reference to Mayor Koch and Westway. That was way too provincial, and made sense in New York City only for a brief time. Outside of New York, it's probably totally inexplicable. I'll have to curb myself of using current references with such short shelf life.

CHERNOBYL, AND THE STORY OF THE TEACHER GETTING SHOT

Chernobyl is less current, but still a name that reverberates; so I'd leave it alone for now.

No one probably remembers the teacher story anymore (which was moderately current when I wrote the play). But I think we can let it remain a story that impressed and bothered the Man. Plus, the audience may assume that it's a current story, which it easily could be.

SHIRLEY MacLAINE

The reference is feeling a little old, but it still works in people's heads and I don't have an idea for a newer person who represents the same popular interest in mystical things. So for now, keep.

A CLARIFICATION ABOUT THE "BALI HAI, KUMBAYA" SECTION

In the Man's speech on the Harmonic Convergence, on page 35, I've seen some actors seemingly not understand this section of his speech. So let me explain.

The Man is disdainful of a teenager who insisted on reciting a song, like a poem. The Man can't remember if it was "Blowin' in the Wind" — the kind of song that might be recited idealistically — or "Bali Hai," the kind of song from Broadway (it's from *South Pacific*) that in no way fits the teenager's desire to be idealistic and profound. Thus the "Bali Hai" reference is a joke the Man is making.

Then, moments later, after feeling "separate" (a serious, sincere moment), the Man tries to get rid of his uncomfortable feeling by doing an affirmation.

He starts the affirmation sincerely ("I am not separate. I am one with the universe"), but he can't throw off his "separate" feeling, so his affirmation starts to turn into a tongue-in-cheek affirmation.

He affirms some things he doubts (guides speaking through Shirley MacLaine). Then he *recites* the out-of-context lyrics to "Bali Hai," making reference thus to the serious teenager whom he found pretentious and who had recited an idealistic song. He then switches to another lyric fragment (the song "They Call the Wind Maria" from *Paint Your Wagon*), and ends up reciting part of the peace-song, "Kumbaya."

It's important that these lyrics are *recited,* not sung; otherwise the connection with these affirmations and the teenager is lost.

I saw an actor play this section by suddenly bursting into singing "Bali Hai" energetically, as if the Man were suddenly an obsessive musical comedy buff. That's not the point or the mood I'm going for, and it was very jarring. (Plus, by singing it, the actor kept us from getting the connection back to the teenager, so that the singing of "Bali Hai" seemed truly an unfunny non-sequitur.)

So please recite the lyrics. This section is a combination of the Man putting down affirmations; of his referring back to the teenager whom he found pretentious; and finally of his drifting back to his sad feeling of disconnection with life, with belief, with the people at the Harmonic Convergence.

So the affirmation starts sincerely ("I am not separate"); moves to playful put-down; and, just around "Kumbaya," gets kind of sad again (even though the reciting of all of these songs is meant to be playful).

Anyway, I can see where this can be misleading. So I hope it feels clearer now.

SOME ACTING NOTES

When this play was published I'd never seen any other actors even audition for the parts because E. Katherine Kerr and I were pre-cast in the Playwrights Horizons production.

Seeing actors audition — and seeing other actors perform a role in a production — often gives me a knowledge of where the play might be confusing to actors.

From the L.A. production on, I've seen other actors, in both performance and auditions. And I now have a few comments I'd like to make about acting the two parts.

I hope you'll take the comments in the spirit of friendly guidance, and you won't instead get your backs up and get all interested in proving me wrong. I'm not actually interested in being right; but I am interested in making sure the audience enjoys the play, and I've seen some interpretations that interfere with that.

REGARDING THE WOMAN'S ROLE

Re-reading all the references to the Woman's having been institutionalized, I want to warn you against playing the Woman as an obvious street crazy or bag lady, with facial tics and crazy panting and so on and on. (I've seen this done in auditions.)

The New York and L.A. production actresses — E. Katherine Kerr and Jean Smart — both intuitively played the Woman as highly intelligent and sardonic; as the play went on and we heard how extreme her opinions were, we started to have our own judgments of how crazy or not crazy the character was. But if you play her as out-front crazy from the first word, audiences stop listening to her opinions — most of which are articulate and interesting, if still "off" — and just watch odd behavior, which fast becomes fatiguing.

I saw one audition where the opening lines about "It's just too difficult to be alive, isn't it? ... there are all these people to deal with" simply did not register as thoughts or sentences. The actress was playing: "I'm unstable; you don't know if I'm going to suddenly shout in a minute; I blink my eyes oddly; I'm a strange presence in the room with you, I come on too strong, etc. etc."

I "got" that she was crazy; but I didn't hear a word she said. Her acting was not in any way about communicating the meaning of the words in her speech; her acting was about communicating a layer she was putting on top, that layer being about the woman's pathological craziness. The strength of the words was meaningless in her interpretation; we stopped listening because she was not making connections between her words and any thoughts behind them. And words said without thought and content behind them become like guttural utterances; and we in the audience become extremely bored with this, fast.

I can see how if you focus on the Woman's having been institutionalized, you can decide that means she's crazy; and you can think you're doing the right thing by "playing crazy."

Both E. Katherine Kerr and Jean Smart played smart women, articulate, even witty. They, though, were in a state of anger and frustration at how the world worked; and they used the words of the script to communicate and explain to the audience why they felt the way they did. In most ways the audience agreed with and identified with the frustrations the Woman expressed.

Plus, don't forget, there are many people who have been institutionalized for periods of time who when you meet them seem quite normal. So don't take the facts of the Woman's institutionalization to mean she is a walking facial tic that screams. Her institutionalization means that she has tenuous connections to reality and to what is appropriate, at the same time she is still able to be smart and articulate.

Part of the humor and tension of the play is when we're left to realize ways in which we don't agree with the Woman, or don't feel safe with her, as time goes by. When she asks if any of us would give her a job, it's an eerie realization that almost no one in the theatre would consider doing so; she's too unstable.

But be unreasonable when the script takes you there (when she envisions Mother Teresa and Dr. Ruth fighting to the death, for instance; or "LET ME BABY-SIT YOUR CHILDREN, I PROMISE I WON'T KILL THEM").

The short advice is: play the content of what she says, don't play some surface intention of "look how crazy and unbalanced I am." <u>Mean the words you say</u>.

REGARDING THE MAN'S ROLE

Actually "Mean what you say" is the quick version advice for him too.

Having seen the play a number of times now, I see that the Man's role is actually harder to do than the Woman's. She really does have a whole character, with incidents and history we can get involved with (she sometimes sleeps in her bathtub; she's been to AA, and misbehaved there; she attempted suicide, etc. etc.).

We learn that the Man works at a magazine, that he's bisexual, that he has a bent toward negative thinking but wants to be positive. Beyond that, we know few incidents in his life, know nothing of what relationships he may have had or tried to have. Mostly what we have are his *opinions* about different issues, expressed in that pessimist-trying-to-be-optimist kind of way.

Since so much of the speech is the Man's opinions disconnected from detail about his life, "Seeking Wild" then, in some regards, is like a performed essay. And unless you've ever given speeches to audience, it's a rather hard acting job to know how to do a performed essay.

So some actors I've seen try to "invent" character and quirks for him ... playing him as overly nerdy, or overly like a forgetful professor. One actor played him as disorganized, dropping his cards on his entrance (which could work, but seemed overly schticky in his interpretation). More damaging, though, this actor then did the first several minutes of the speech in a bad and unfriendly mood because he "decided" that the Man had just nearly been run over by a bicycle right before the speech started.

Since nowhere does the script say that the bicycle incident has just happened, the audience had no idea what he was doing — all they got was that he seemed distracted and grouchy. They got that color, but they didn't really hear or hook into what his words were saying about once he was negative, now he was trying to be positive. The acting decision he made actually fought the content of the words.

So, unless you're an actor who's brilliant at creating character away from your own persona (like Kevin Kline or Meryl Streep), I would instead urge you to play the part using your own persona. Don't invent character quirks. Play it as yourself; act as if you had the same opinions as those stated in the play. Really mean what you say. Be sincere.

It's your commitment to what you're saying that will hold the audience's attention, and will let the words be of interest to them. When you're upset and in disagreement about the Supreme Court ruling about homosexuals, then mean those words. That's where the acting comes in this piece. It doesn't come from saying the lines about the Supreme Court, while all the time actually acting you have a stone in your shoe, or you're mad at a bicycle rider that you're not presently talking about. Relate to the words the character says.

Meaning everything you say is the actual acting task. Mean what you say when you say it. When you equivocate a moment later, well, mean that equivocation too. Let the words work for you. (The way the man seems totally positive one minute, and totally negative the next — and sincere both times — is where some of the comedy arises.)

Also, don't hold onto the words. The Man's speech is wordy, don't cherish all the words. Always be going for the end of the sentence ... the Man is making points. Move towards the point always. High energy is important.

I think the Man genuinely wants to be positive. And so at those moments where he succeeds, that can be a very bright emotional color. Connect with the audience; assume they're going to be your friend. The Man's likeability to the audience is important, so he can bring them along with his opinions.

Finally, though the Man may find anger in the speech at certain logical times, please don't decide he's generally an angry person ... he's more of a comical, put-upon person. The Woman has so much anger in her, that if the Man has it too, the play becomes all off-balance.

But mostly: mean what you say.

Thanks for listening. Good luck. I hope the play is fun to put on.

BRIEF UPDATE ON ESSAY ON CRITICS IN NEW YORK

I received many nice and encouraging letters after my essay appeared at the end of *Laughing Wild*. I thank the people who wrote me.

I don't feel I have anything to take back from what I said, though the essay seemed to give rise to a rumor that I stopped writing "because" of Frank Rich. This was partially true, partially untrue. As the essay reflected accurately, I found his frequently dismissive response to my work was, indeed, making me dread presenting a play in New York; and from 1988 to 1993 I did not.

But looking back, it wasn't only that which was stopping me. I think I was in a kind of writer's block during that time. Totally disconnected to Rich, I just wasn't feeling the "impulse" to write. I'm happy to say that sometime in 1993 the impulse returned; in 1994 I presented an evening of one acts at the Manhattan Theatre Club called DURANG/DURANG; and I've written a new play on commission for Lincoln Center called SEX AND LONGING, which is scheduled to be presented in fall 1996. And I have an act done of another play.

So my silence for several years came about from something within my own spirit as much as from my frustration with critics.

Oddly, in 1993, I was just moving to the psychological space of accepting the critical situation and be willing to brave writing for New York theatre again when Rich on his own retired from the theatre page and moved to editorial writing on the op-ed page of the *Times*.

With the new critics of the *Times,* there remains the continuing problem of the *Times'* too-strong voice. But personally at least, I don't have a history, negative or positive, with these particular critics, and so I don't feel as doomed-from-the-start. (And the response to DURANG/DURANG was very welcoming from all the critics, which I must admit was a nice feeling.)

So I'm writing again. I wish my Harvard classmate Mr. Rich (though I didn't know him there) well in his new position — legitimately I do, he's a very good writer — and I'm planning to pay less attention to criticism, positive or negative, in the future. As Stephen Sondheim says in *Sunday in the Park with George*: "Move on."

Christopher Durang
January 1996

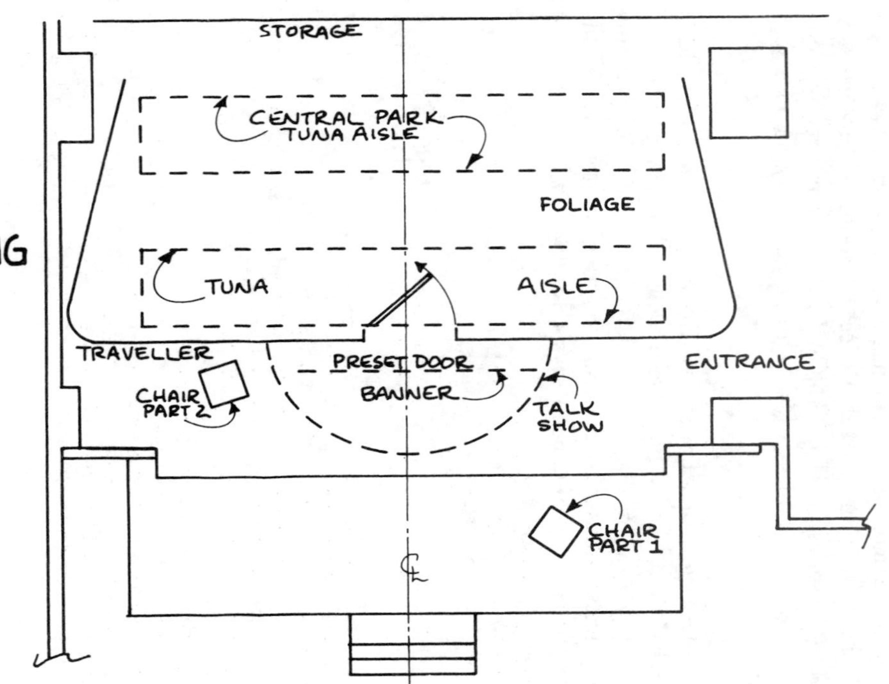
SCENE DESIGN
"LAUGHING WILD"
STORAGE
CENTRAL PARK
TUNA AISLE
FOLIAGE
TUNA
AISLE
TRAVELLER
PRESET DOOR
BANNER
ENTRANCE
CHAIR
PART 2
TALK
SHOW
CHAIR
PART 1

NEW PLAYS

• **SMASH by Jeffrey Hatcher.** Based on the novel, AN UNSOCIAL SOCIALIST by George Bernard Shaw, the story centers on a millionaire Socialist who leaves his bride on their wedding day because he fears his passion for her will get in the way of his plans to overthrow the British government. *"SMASH is witty, cunning, intelligent, and skillful."* *–Seattle Weekly. "SMASH is a wonderfully high-style British comedy of manners that evokes the world of Shaw's high-minded heroes and heroines, but shaped by a post modern sensibility." –Seattle Herald.* [5M, 5W] ISBN: 0-8222-1553-5

• **PRIVATE EYES by Steven Dietz.** A comedy of suspicion in which nothing is ever quite what it seems. *"Steven Dietz's ... Pirandellian smooch to the mercurial nature of theatrical illusion and romantic truth, Dietz's spiraling structure and breathless pacing provide enough of an oxygen rush to revive any moribund audience member ... Dietz's mastery of playmaking ... is cause for kudos." –The Village Voice. "The cleverest and most artful piece presented at the 21st annual [Humana] festival was PRIVATE EYES by writer-director Steven Dietz." –The Chicago Tribune.* [3M, 2W] ISBN: 0-8222-1619-1

• **DIMLY PERCEIVED THREATS TO THE SYSTEM by Jon Klein.** Reality and fantasy overlap with hilarious results as this unforgettable family attempts to survive the nineties. *"Here's a play whose point about fractured families goes to the heart, mind -- and ears." –The Washington Post. " ... an end-of-the millennium comedy about a family on the verge of a nervous breakdown ... Trenchant and hilarious ... " –The Baltimore Sun.* [2M, 4W] ISBN: 0-8222-1677-9

• **HONOUR by Joanna Murray-Smith.** In a series of intense confrontations, a wife, husband, lover and daughter negotiate the forces of passion, lust, history, responsibility and honour. *"Tight, crackling dialogue (usually played out in punchy verbal duels) captures characters unable to deal with emotions ... Murray-Smith effectively places her characters in situations that strip away pretense." –Variety. "HONOUR might just capture a few honors of its own." –Time Out Magazine.* [1M, 3W] ISBN: 0-8222-1683-3

• **NINE ARMENIANS by Leslie Ayvazian.** A revealing portrait of three generations of an Armenian-American family. *" ... Ayvazian's obvious personal exploration ... is evocative, and her picture of an American Life colored nostalgically by an increasingly alien ethnic tradition, is persuasively embedded into a script of a certain supple grace ... " –The NY Post. "... NINE ARMENIANS is a warm, likable work that benefits from ... Ayvazian's clear-headed insight into the dynamics of a close-knit family ... " –Variety.* [5M, 5W] ISBN: 0-8222-1602-7

• **PSYCHOPATHIA SEXUALIS by John Patrick Shanley.** Fetishes and psychiatry abound in this scathing comedy about a man and his father's argyle socks. *"John Patrick Shanley's new play, PSYCHOPATHIA SEXUALIS is ... perfectly poised between daffy comedy and believable human neurosis which Shanley combines so well ... " –The LA Times. "John Patrick Shanley's PSYCHOPATHIA SEXUALIS is a salty boulevard comedy with a bittersweet theme ... " –New York Magazine. "A tour de force of witty, barbed dialogue." –Variety.* [3M, 2W] ISBN: 0-8222-1615-9

NEW PLAYS

• **A QUESTION OF MERCY by David Rabe.** The Obie Award-winning playwright probes the sensitive and controversial issue of doctor-assisted suicide in the age of AIDS in this poignant drama. *"There are many devastating ironies in Mr. Rabe's beautifully considered, piercingly clear-eyed work ... " –The NY Times. "With unsettling candor and disturbing insight, the play arouses pity and understanding of a troubling subject ... Rabe's provocative tale is an affirmation of dignity that rings clear and true." –Variety.* [6M, 1W] ISBN: 0-8222-1643-4

• **A DOLL'S HOUSE by Henrik Ibsen, adapted by Frank McGuinness. Winner of the 1997 Tony Award for best revival.** *"New, raw, gut-twisting and gripping. Easily the hottest drama this season." –USA Today. "Bold, brilliant and alive." –The Wall Street Journal. "A thunderclap of an evening that takes your breath away." –Time. "The stuff of Broadway legend." –Associated Press.* [4M, 4W, 2 boys] ISBN: 0-8222-1636-1

• **THE WAITING ROOM by Lisa Loomer.** Three women from different centuries meet in a doctor's waiting room in this dark comedy about the timeless quest for beauty -- and its cost. *" ... THE WAITING ROOM ... is a bold, risky melange of conflicting elements that is ... terrifically moving ... There's no resisting the fierce emotional pull of the play." –The NY Times. " ... one of the high points of this year's Off-Broadway season ... THE WAITING ROOM is well worth a visit." –Back Stage.* [7M, 4W, flexible casting] ISBN: 0-8222-1594-2

• **MR. PETERS' CONNECTIONS by Arthur Miller.** Mr. Miller describes the protagonist as existing in a dream-like state when the mind is "freed to roam from real memories to conjectures, from trivialities to tragic insights, from terror of death to glorying in one's being alive." With this memory play, the Tony Award and Pulitzer Prize-winner reaffirms his stature as the world's foremost dramatist. *" ... a cross between Joycean stream-of-consciousness and Strindberg's dream plays, sweetened with a dose of William Saroyan's philosophical whimsy ... CONNECTIONS is most intriguing ... Miller scholars will surely find many connections of their own to make between this work and the author's earlier plays." –The NY Times.* [5M, 3W] ISBN: 0-8222-1687-6

• **THE STEWARD OF CHRISTENDOM by Sebastian Barry.** A freely imagined portrait of the author's great-grandfather, the last Chief Superintendent of the Dublin Metropolitan Police. *"MAGNIFICENT ... the cool, elegiac eye of James Joyce's THE DEAD; the bleak absurdity of Samuel Beckett's lost, primal characters; the cosmic anger of KING LEAR ..." –The NY Times. "Sebastian Barry's compassionate imaging of an ancestor he never knew is among the most poignant onstage displays of humanity in recent memory." –Variety.* [5M, 4W] ISBN: 0-8222-1609-4

• **SYMPATHETIC MAGIC by Lanford Wilson. Winner of the 1997 Obie for best play.** The mysteries of the universe, and of human and artistic creation, are explored in this award-winning play. *"Lanford Wilson's idiosyncratic SYMPATHETIC MAGIC is his BEST PLAY YET ... the rare play you WANT ... chock-full of ideas, incidents, witty or poetic lines, scientific and philosophical argument ... you'll find your intellectual faculties racing." –New York Magazine. "The script is like a fully notated score, next to which most new plays are cursory lead sheets." –The Village Voice.* [5M, 3W] ISBN: 0-8222-1630-2